D1147513

FIFTY MAJOR DOCUMENTS

of the Nineteenth Century

D
351
S55
1977

LOUIS L. SNYDER

Professor of History
City University of New York

THE ANVIL SERIES

under the general editorship of
LOUIS L. SNYDER

ROBERT E. KRIEGER PUBLISHING COMPANY
HUNTINGTON, NEW YORK

Original Edition 1955
Reprint Edition 1979

Printed and Published by
ROBERT E. KRIEGER PUBLISHING COMPANY, INC.
645 NEW YORK AVENUE
HUNTINGTON, NEW YORK 11743

Library of Congress Cataloging in Publication Data

Snyder, Louis Leo, 1907-   editor
    Fifty major documents of the nineteenth century.

    Reprint of the edition published by D. Van Nostrand
Co., Princeton, N.J., which was issued as no. 10 of An Anvil
original.
    1. History, Modern—19th century—Sources.   I. Title.
[D351.S55   1979]   909.82   78-10792
ISBN 0-88275-751-2

National Series Data Program
ISSN #0570-1062

PREFACE

This volume is the outcome of the gratifying reception accorded another Anvil book: *Fifty Major Documents of the Twentieth Century*. Both collections are based on the belief that the raw materials out of which the compressed treatment of many books is constructed should be consulted by both students and the general reader. The purpose is to present the basic and most important documents essential to an understanding of the century without the utilization of unnecessary spacefillers characteristic of many massive textbooks.

It will be noted that the term "Documents" is used not in the German sense of *Akten* but in the more general sense of source material, mainly official documents, but including also contemporary accounts and eyewitness descriptions. The selections have been grouped under fifty headings, but the total runs to nearly twice that number. Each selection presents, as far as possible, a specific historical event, idea, or trend. Introductory notes serve to connect the documents and to explain the historical framework surrounding the event.

The editor is under no illusion that these selections represent the last word on the most important documents of the nineteenth century. He has attempted on the basis of his own experience and the advice of colleagues to include the most significant ones. In the final analysis, any such compilation must be highly personal in nature. Other historians would undoubtedly compile a somewhat different collection. But it is hoped that this group of documents will serve to give the reader an insight into the scope and the significance of a century in which tremendous transformations took place in world history.

The editor wishes to express his thanks to Wallace Sokolsky, colleague and friend, who made many valuable suggestions for this book.

Louis L. Snyder

TABLE OF CONTENTS

JEFFERSON'S FIRST INAUGURAL ADDRESS, MARCH 4, 1801 [1]

President Thomas Jefferson's first inaugural was the first such ceremony held at Washington, where the permanent capital had been established in 1800. The President-elect came to Washington, stayed at a boarding-house, and on noon of March 4th, 1801, like any private citizen walked to Capitol Hill. His inaugural address, one of the great state papers of American history, is a classic exposition of democratic philosophy. In noble and moving passages, the new President emphasized the necessity for a government of limited powers, recognition of the rights of state governments, economy in the national administration, political and religious tolerance, "honest friendship with all nations, entangling alliances with none," the supremacy of the civil over the military authorities, and the rights of popular election. This confession of faith, which sank deeply into the minds of the people, has remained to this day the ideal of the American way of life.

✓   ✓   ✓

Friends and Fellow-Citizens:

Called upon to undertake the duties of the first executive office of our country, I avail myself of the presence of that portion of my fellow-citizens which is here assembled to express my grateful thanks for the favor

[1] James D. Richardson, ed., *Compilation of the Messages and Papers of the Presidents, 1789-1897* (Washington, 1896-99), I, 322 ff.

which they have been pleased to look toward me, to declare a sincere consciousness that the task is above my talents, and that I approach it with those anxious and awful presentiments which the greatness of the charge and the weakness of my powers so justly inspire. A rising nation, spread over a wide and fruitful land, traversing all the seas with the rich productions of their industry, engaged in commerce with nations who feel power and forget right, advancing rapidly to destinies beyond the reach of mortal eye—when I contemplate these transcendent objects, and see the honor, the happiness, and the hopes of this beloved country committed to the issue and the auspices of this day, I shrink from the contemplation, and humble myself before the magnitude of the undertaking. Utterly, indeed, should I despair did not the presence of many whom I see here remind me that in the other high authorities provided by our Constitution I shall find resources of wisdom, of virtue, and of zeal on which to rely under all difficulties. To you, then, gentlemen, who are charged with the sovereign functions of legislation, and to those associated with you, I look with encouragement for that guidance and support which may enable us to steer with safety the vessel in which we are all embarked amidst the conflicting elements of a troubled world.

During the contest of opinion through which we have passed the animation of discussions and of exertions has sometimes worn an aspect which might impose on strangers unused to think freely and to speak and write what they think; but this being now decided by the voice of the nation, announced according to the rules of the Constitution, all will, of course, arrange themselves under the will of the law, and unite in common efforts for the common good. All, too, will bear in mind this sacred principle, that though the will of the majority is in all cases to prevail, that will to be rightful must be reasonable; that the minority possess their equal rights, which equal law must protect, and to violate would be oppression. Let us, then, fellow-citizens, unite with one heart and one mind. Let us restore to social intercourse that harmony and affection without which liberty and even life itself are but dreary things. And let us reflect that, having banished from our land that religious intolerance under which mankind so long bled and suffered, we have yet gained little if we countenance a political intolerance as despotic, as wicked, and capable of as bitter and bloody persecutions.

During the throes and convulsions of the ancient world, during the agonizing spasms of infuriated man, seeking through blood and slaughter his long-lost liberty, it was not wonderful that the agitation of the billows should reach even this distant and peaceful shore; that this should be more felt and feared by some and less by others, and should divide opinions as to measures of safety. But every difference of opinion is not a difference of principle. We have called by different names brethren of the same principle. We are all Republicans, we are all Federalists.

If there be any among us who would wish to dissolve this Union or to change its republican form, let them stand undisturbed as monuments of the safety with which error of opinion may be tolerated where reason is left free to combat it. I know, indeed, that some honest men fear that a republican government cannot be strong, that this government is not strong enough; but would the honest patriot, in the full tide of successful experiment, abandon a government which has so far kept us free and firm on the theoretic and visionary fear that this Government, the world's best hope, may by possibility want energy to preserve itself? I trust not. I believe this, on the contrary, the strongest Government on earth. I believe it the only one where every man, at the call of the law, would fly to the standard of the law, and would meet invasions of the public order as his own personal concern. Sometimes it is said that man can not be trusted with the government of himself. Can he, then, be trusted with the government of others? Or have we found angels in the forms of kings to govern him? Let history answer this question.

Let us, then, with courage and confidence pursue our own Federal and Republican principles, our attachment to union and representative government. Kindly separated by nature and a wide ocean from the exterminating havoc of one-quarter of the globe; too high-minded to endure the degradations of the others; possessing a chosen country, with room enough for our descendants to the thousandth and thousandth generation; entertaining a due sense of our equal right to the use of our own faculties, to the acquisitions of our own industry, to honor and confidence from our fellow-citizens, resulting not from birth, but from our actions and their sense of them; enlightened by a benign religion, professed, indeed, and practiced in various forms, yet all of them inculcating honesty, truth, temperance, gratitude, and the love of man; acknowledging and adoring an overruling Providence, which by all its dispensations proves that it delights in the happiness of man here and his greater happiness hereafter—with all these blessings, what more is necessary to make us a happy and prosperous people? Still one thing more, fellow-citizens—a wise and frugal Government, which shall restrain men from injuring one another, shall leave them otherwise free to regulate their own pursuits of industry and improvement, and shall not take from the mouth of labor the bread it has earned. This is the sum of good government, and this is necessary to close the circle of our felicities.

About to enter, fellow-citizens, on the exercise of duties which comprehend everything dear and valuable to you, it is proper you should understand what I deem the essential principles of our Government, and consequently those which ought to shape its Administration. I will compress them within the narrowest compass they will bear, stating the general principle, but not all its limitations. Equal and exact justice to all men, of whatever state or persuasion, religious or political; peace, commerce, and honest friendship with all nations, entangling alliances with none; the support of the State governments in all their rights, as the most competent administrations for our domestic concerns and the surest bulwarks against antirepublican tendencies; the preservation of the General Government in its whole constitutional vigor, as the sheet anchor of our peace at home and safety abroad; a jealous care of the right of election by the people—a mild and safe corrective of abuses which are lopped by the sword of revolution where peaceable remedies are unprovided; absolute acquiescence in the

decisions of the majority, the vital principle of republics, from which is no appeal but to force, the vital principle and immediate parent of despotism; a well-disciplined militia, our best reliance in peace and for the first moments of war, till regulars may relieve them; the supremacy of the civil over the military authority; economy in the public expense, that labor may be lightly burthened; the honest payment of our debts and sacred preservation of the public faith; encouragement of agriculture, and of commerce as its handmaiden; the diffusion of information and arraignment of all abuses at the bar of public reason; freedom of religion; freedom of the press, and freedom of person under the protection of the habeas corpus, and trial by juries impartially selected.

These principles form the bright constellation which has gone before us and guided our steps through an age of revolution and reformation. The wisdom of our sages and blood of our heroes have been devoted to their attainment. They should be the creed of our political faith, the text of civic instruction, the touchstone by which we try the services of those we trust; and should we wander from them in moments of error or alarm, let us hasten to retrace our steps and to regain the road which alone leads to peace, liberty, and safety.

I repair, then, fellow-citizens, to the post you have assigned to me. With experience enough in subordinate offices to have seen the difficulties of this the greatest of all, I have learnt to expect that it will rarely fall to the lot of imperfect man to retire from this station with the reputation and the favor which bring him into it. Without pretentions to that high confidence you reposed in our first and greatest revolutionary character, whose preëminent services had entitled him to the first place in his country's love and destined for him the fairest page in the volume of faithful history, I ask so much confidence only as may give firmness and effect to the legal administration of your affairs. I shall often go wrong through defect of judgment. When right, I shall often be thought wrong by those whose positions will not command a view of the whole ground. I ask your indulgence for my own errors, which will never be

intentional, and your support against the errors of others, who may condemn· what they would not if seen in all its parts. The approbation implied by your suffrage is a great consolation to me for the past, and my future solicitude will be to retain the good opinion of those who have bestowed it in advance, to conciliate that of others by doing them all the good in my power, and to be instrumental to the happiness and freedom of all.

Relying, then, on the patronage of your good will, I advance with obedience to the work, ready to retire from it whenever you have become sensible how much better choice it is in your power to make. And may that Infinite Power which rules the destinies of the universe lead our councils to what is best, and give them a favorable issue for your peace and prosperity.

— 2 —

NAPOLEON'S SALE OF LOUISIANA TO THE UNITED STATES, APRIL 30, 1803

In 1762, France, by the Treaty of Fontainebleu, ceded Louisiana west cf the Mississippi to Spain. In 1800, by the secret Treaty of St. Ildefonso, Spain gave the territory back to France. Concerned about the new powerful neighbor along the Mississippi, President Jefferson requested the American minister to France, Robert R. Livingston, to ascertain the terms on which French would sell the territory to the United States. "Every eye is now fixed on the affairs of Louisiana," Jefferson wrote the ambassador. "Perhaps nothing since the revolutionary war has produced more uneasy sensations through the body of the nation."

Fearing that at any moment England would renew the great war against him, Napoleon was anxious to convert the liability of Louisiana into an asset—money to carry on war against Britain. He sold the territory for approximately eleven million dollars. "I have just given England," he said, "a maritime rival that sooner or later will lay low her pride." Although under the French Constitution Napoleon had no right to sell Louisiana without the approval of his legislature, he went ahead in characteristic contempt for democratic controls.

Jefferson, too, lacked written authority in the Constitution to acquire new land. But this was no time for consistency. He advised the Senate to ratify the agreement before Bonaparte changed his mind. "The less said about any constitutional difficulty, the better."

In following Hamilton's doctrine of implied powers in this action Jefferson was ultimately supported by the Supreme Court. It was the greatest single achievement of Jefferson's administration, one of the most decisive actions in modern times, and certainly the real-estate bargain of all time.

✓   ✓   ✓

The Convention of April 30, 1803 [2]

ARTICLE 1. *Whereas,* by the article the third of the treaty concluded at St. Ildefonso, the 1st October, 1800 between the First Consul of the French Republic and his Catholic Majesty, it was agreed as follows: "His Catholic Majesty promises and engages on his part, to cede to the French Republic, six months after the full and entire execution of the conditions and stipulations herein relative to his royal highness the duke of Parma, the colony or province of Louisiana, with the same extent that it had when France possessed it; and such as it should be after the treaties subsequently entered into between Spain and other states." And *whereas,* in pursuance of the Treaty, and particularly of the third ar-

[2] William W. Malloy, ed., *Treaties, Conventions, International Acts, Protocols and Agreements between the United States of America and other Powers* (3 vols., Washington, 1910-23), I, 508 ff.

ticle, the French Republic has an incontestable title to the domain and to the possession of the said territory: —The First Consul of the French Republic desiring to give to the United States a strong proof of his friendship, both hereby cede to the said United States, in the name of the French Republic, forever and in full sovereignty, the said territory with all its rights and appurtenances, as fully and in the same manner as they have been acquired by the French Republic, in virtue of the above mentioned Treaty, concluded with his Catholic Majesty.

ARTICLE 2. In the cession made by the preceding article are included the adjacent islands belonging to Louisiana, all public lots and squares, vacant lands, and all public buildings, fortifications, barracks, and other edifices which are not private property.—The Archives, papers, and documents, relative to the domain and sovereignty of Louisiana, and its dependencies, will be left in the possession of the Commissaries of the United States, and copies will be afterwards given in due form to the Magistrates and Municipal officers, of such of the said papers and documents as may be necessary to them.

ARTICLE 3. The inhabitants of the ceded territory shall be incorporated in the Union of the United States, and admitted as soon as possible, according to the principles of the Federal Constitution, to the enjoyment of all the rights, advantages, and immunities of citizens of the United States, and in the meantime they shall be maintained and protected in the free enjoyment of their liberty, property, and the Religion which they profess. . . .

ARTICLE 9. The particular Convention signed this day by the respective Ministers having for its object to provide for the payment of debts due to the citizens of the United States by the French Republic prior to the 30th September 1800 (8th Vendémiaire and 9) is approved and to have its execution in the same manner as if it had been inserted in this present treaty and it shall be ratified in the same form and in the same time so that the one shall not be ratified distinct from the other.

Another particular Convention signed at the same date as the present treaty relative to a definitive rule between the contracting parties is in the like manner approved and will be ratified in the same form, and in the same time jointly.

— 3 —

DISSOLUTION OF THE HOLY ROMAN EMPIRE, AUGUST 6, 1806

On December 2, 1805, Napoleon won one of the most celebrated of his many victories when he defeated the combined Austrian and Russian armies at Austerlitz. Emperor Francis II was forced to sign the Treaty of Pressburg, whereby he returned his Venetian territories to Napoleon's Kingdom of Italy. The peace further recognized the rulers of Bavaria and Württemberg and the Elector of Baden as independent of the Holy Roman Emperor. On July 12, 1806, Napoleon set up the Confederation of the Rhine "forever separated from the territory of the Germanic Empire," and on August 1st sent a brusque message to the Imperial Diet announcing the end of the Holy Roman Empire. Five days later Francis II abdicated as Holy Roman Emperor, but retained the title of Francis I, Emperor of Austria.

Thus, the old Holy Roman Empire, which had been the only bond linking the Germanies together for more than eight hundred years since the imperial coronation by the Pope of Otto I in 962, disappeared, and the legal existence of the German states that had grown up on its territory was recognized. This consolidation of the Germanies survived Napoleon's downfall, and paved the way for Germany's national unification.

A

Napoleon's Note to the Imperial Diet, August 1, 1806 [3]

The undersigned, *chargé d'affaires* of His Majesty the Emperor of the French and King of Italy at the Diet of the German Empire, has been ordered by His Majesty to make the following declaration to the Diet:

Their Majesties the Kings of Bavaria and of Württemberg, the Sovereign Princes of Regensburg, Baden, Berg, Hesse-Darmstadt and Nassau, and the other leading Princes of the south and west of Germany have resolved to form a confederation among themselves which shall protect them against future emergencies. They have thus ceased to be States of the Empire.

The position in which the Treaty of Pressburg has specifically placed the courts in alliance with France, and indirectly those Princes whose lands they border or surround, being incompatible with the existence of the Empire, it thus becomes necessary for those rulers to reorganize their relations on a new basis and to eliminate a contradiction that could not fail to be a permanent source of agitation, unrest, and danger. . . .

The Diet no longer has a will of its own. The judgments of the superior law courts can no longer be executed. There is such serious weakness that the federal bond no longer gives any protection and only means a source of dissension and discord between the powers. . . .

His Majesty the Emperor and King is, therefore, compelled to state that he can no longer recognize the existence of the German Constitution. He acknowledges, however, the complete and absolute sovereignty of each of the Princes whose States compose Germany today, and maintains with them the same relations as with the other independent Powers of Europe.

His Majesty the Emperor and King has accepted the title: *Protector of the Confederation of the Rhine.* He has been motivated solely by the interests of peace, so

[3] A.J.H. and Jules de Clercq, *Receuil des traités de la France, publié sous les auspices du ministère des affaires étrangères* (Paris, 1864-1917), II, 183-84.

that by his constant mediation between the weak and the powerful he may avoid every kind of disorder and dissension. . . .

His Majesty stated that he would never extend the limits of France beyond the Rhine. His sole aim now is to so employ the means which Providence has confided in him that the freedom of the seas may be maintained, and the liberty of commerce, and thus assure the peace and happiness of mankind.

Regensburg, August 1, 1806.

BACHER

B

Abdication of Francis II, August 6, 1806 [4]

We, Francis the Second, by the Grace of God Roman Emperor Elect, Ever August, Hereditary Emperor of Austria, etc., King of Germany, Hungary, Bohemia, Croatia, Dalmatia, Slavonia, Galizia, Lodomeria and Jerusalem, Archduke of Austria, etc.

Since the Peace of Pressburg all our care and attention has been directed to the purpose of fulfilling carefully all the provisions of the said treaty, as well as the preservation of peace so necessary to the happiness of our subjects, and the strengthening in every way of the friendly relations now so happily established. We could but await the outcome of events in order to decide whether the significant changes in the German Empire resulting from the peace terms would permit us to fulfill the weighty duties which devolve upon us as head of the Empire. But the results of certain articles of the Treaty of Pressburg . . . have convinced us that it would be impossible under these circumstances further to fulfill the duties which we have assumed by the conditions of our election. . . .

Thus, convinced of the utter impossibility of any longer fulfilling the duties of our Imperial office, we owe it to our principles and honor to renounce a crown which could only have value in our eyes so long as we were in a position to justify the confidence placed in us by the Electors, Princes, estates, and other members of the German Empire, and to fulfill the duties devolving upon us.

[4] *Moniteur,* August 14, 1806.

We proclaim, therefore, that we consider the ties which have thus far united us to the German Empire as dissolved; that we look upon the office and dignity of the Imperial headship as dissolved by the formation of a separate federation of the Rhenish States, and regard ourselves as freed from all obligations to the German Empire. Herewith we lay down the Imperial crown which is associated with such obligations and we relinquish the Imperial Government which we have thus far conducted. . . .

Done at our capital and royal residence, Vienna, August 6, 1806, in the 15th year of our reign as Emperor and hereditary ruler of the Austrian lands.

FRANCIS

— 4 —

NAPOLEON'S CONTINENTAL SYSTEM, 1806-07

Napoleon's fall was closely related to his failure to challenge successfully the British supremacy on the seas. The British naval victory of Trafalgar on October 21, 1805 made it imperative for Napoleon to compensate for his lack of naval power by destroying British commerce. Contemptuously labeling the English "a nation of shopkeepers," he inaugurated the so-called "Continental System" with the Berlin Decree of November 21, 1806 designed to cut England off from all her Continental trade.

The British straightway retaliated with an Order in Council of January 10, 1807 and another on November 11, 1807, which forbade neutral trade and created a blockade of all Britain's enemies. Napoleon, in turn, answered with the Milan Decree of December 17, 1807, which declared that any neutral ship obeying the British orders was subject to seizure.

Napoleon had not foreseen the complex results of this economic warfare. Even he could not produce overnight for his army fifty thousand overcoats, which, by devious roundabout means, came from the British factories to the backs of French soldiers. England actually prospered during this contest of economic endurance. Smugglers on the Continent reaped a rich harvest, while merchants and workers, hard hit by the cessation of trade, were reduced to poverty. Throughout the Continent the French conqueror was held responsible for the widespread economic ruin.

✓   ✓   ✓

A

The Berlin Decree, November 21, 1806 [5]

ARTICLE 1. The British islands are declared in a state of blockade.

ARTICLE 2. All commerce and correspondence with the British islands are prohibited. In consequence, letters or packets, addressed either to England, to an Englishman, or in the English language, shall not pass through the post-office and shall be seized.

ARTICLE 3. Every subject of England, of whatever rank and condition soever, who shall be found in the countries occupied by our troops, or by those of our allies, shall be made a prisoner of war.

ARTICLE 4. All magazines, merchandise, or property whatsoever, belonging to England, or coming from its manufactories and colonies, is declared lawful prize.

ARTICLE 5. The trade in English merchandise is forbidden; all merchandise belonging to England, or coming from its manufactories and colonies, is declared lawful prize.

ARTICLE 6. One half of the proceeds of the confiscation of the merchandise and property, declared good prize by the preceding articles, shall be applied to indemnify the merchants for the losses which they have suffered by the capture of merchant vessels by English cruisers.

ARTICLE 7. No vessel coming directly from England,

[5] *State Papers and Public Documents of the United States,* V, 478.

or from the English colonies, or having been there since the publication of the present decree, shall be received into any port.

ARTICLE 8. Every vessel contravening the above clause, by means of a false declaration, shall be seized, and the vessel and cargo confiscated, as if they were English property.

ARTICLE 9. Our tribunal of prizes at Paris is charged with the definitive adjudication of all the controversies, which by the French army, relative to the execution of the present decree. Our tribunal of prizes at Milan shall be charged with the definitive adjudication of the said controversies, which may arise within the extent of our kingdom of Italy.

ARTICLE 10. The present decree shall be communicated to our minister of exterior relations, to the kings of Spain, of Naples, of Holland, and of Etruria, and to our allies, whose subjects, like ours, are the victims of the injustice and the barbarism of the English maritime laws. Our finances, our police, and our post masters general, are charged each, in what concerns him, with the execution of the present decree.

B

The Milan Decree, December 17, 1807 [6]

NAPOLEON, emperor of the French, king of Italy, and protector of the Rhenish confederation.

Observing the measures adopted by the British government, on the 11th November last, by which vessels belonging to neutral, friendly, or even powers the allies of England, are made liable, not only to be searched by English cruisers, but to be compulsorily detained in England, and to have a tax laid on them of so much per cent on the cargo, to be regulated by the British legislature.

Observing that by these acts the British government *denationalizes* ships of every nation in Europe, that it is not competent for any government to detract from its own independence and rights, all the sovereigns of Europe having in trust the sovereignties and independence of the

[6] *State Papers and Public Documents of the United States,* VI, 74.

flag; that if by an unpardonable weakness, and which in the eyes of posterity would be an indelible stain, if such a tyranny was allowed to be established into principles, and consecrated by usage, the English would avail themselves of it to assert it as a right, as they have availed themselves of the tolerance of government to establish the infamous principle, that the flag of a nation does not cover goods, and to have to their right of blockade an arbitrary extension, and which infringes on the sovereignty of every state; we have decreed and do decree as follows:

ARTICLE 1. Every ship, to whatever nation it may belong, that shall have submitted to be searched by an English ship, or to a voyage to England, or shall have paid any tax whatsoever to the English government, is thereby and for that alone, declared to be *denationalized*, to have forfeited the protection of its king, and to have become English property.

ARTICLE 2. Whether the ships thus *denationalized* by the arbitrary measures of the English government, enter into our ports, or those of our allies, or whether they fall into the hands of our ships of war, or of our privateers, they are declared to be good and lawful prize.

ARTICLE 3. The British islands are declared to be in a state of blockade, both by land and sea. Every ship, of whatever nation, or whatsoever the nature of its cargo may be, that sails from the ports of England, of those of the English colonies, and of the countries occupied by English troops, and proceeding to England or to the English colonies, or to countries occupied by English troops, is good and lawful prize, as contrary to the present decree, and may be captured by our ships of war, or our privateers, and adjudged to the captor.

ARTICLE 4. These measures, which are resorted to only in just retaliation of the barbarous system adopted by England, which assimilates its legislation to that of Algiers, shall cease to have any effect with respect to all nations who shall have the firmness to compel the English government to respect their flag. They shall continue to be rigorously in force as long as that government does not return to the principle of the law of nations, which regulates the relations of civilized states in a state of war. The provisions of the present decree shall be abrogated and null, in fact, as soon as the English abide again by the principle of the law of nations, which are also the principles of justice and of honour.

All our ministers are charged with the execution of the present decree, which shall be inserted in the bulletin of the laws.

NAPOLEON

— 5 —

FICHTE'S *ADDRESSES TO THE GERMAN NATION*, 1807-08 [7]

The winter of 1807-08 marked a low point in German morale. Napoleon had occupied Berlin and, at Tilsit, near the Russian border, had concluded a peace, by which Prussia ceded all her territories west of the Elbe. During this dark period, which saw the beginning of German political nationalism, Johann Gottlieb Fichte (1762-1814) delivered in Berlin fourteen addresses to the German people (Reden an die deutsche Nation). In passionate words the philosopher reminded his hearers that their German forefathers had refused to be dominated by the Romans. He urged them to forget their present submission to Napoleon, to believe in themselves, and to understand their great historical mission

Fichte's Addresses, linking love of liberty with national aspiration, were, in effect, a strong plea for German nationalism rather than Prussian or Austrian patriotism. They played an important role in the development of nineteenth-century German nationalism. "In the century that

[7] Johann Gottlieb von Fichte, *Werke* (6 vols.; Leipzig, n.d.), Fritz Medicus Edition, pp. 365-611, *passim.*

separates us from them," Friedrich Meinecke wrote in 1908, "they have never been kept secret, but have been published, read, and become famous as one of the greatest beacons of our new German history."

✓   ✓   ✓

Fichte on German Liberty

Our earliest common ancestors, the primordial stock of the new culture, the Germans, as the Romans called them, courageously resisted the world domination of the Romans. Did they not recognize the superior brilliance of the nearby Roman provinces and the more refined enjoyments in those provinces as well as the abundance of laws, judges' seats, lictors' axes and rods? Is it not true that the Romans were more than willing to allow them to share in these blessings? Did not several of their own princes, who believed that war against such benefactors of mankind was rebellion, experience rewards of the highly praised Roman spirit of clemency? Those who submitted to the Romans were given such marks of distinction as kingly titles, high rank in the armies, and Roman fillets. If their countrymen drove them away, were they not given refuge and subsistence in the colonies by the Romans? Is it possible that they had no appreciation of the advantages of the Roman civilization, for example, of the superior organization of their armies, in which even an Arminius did not let pass the opportunity to learn the trade of war? They cannot be accused rightly of ignorance or want of consideration of any of these things.

The descendants [*of these Germans*], as soon as they could do so without losing their freedom, even went so far as to assimilate the Roman culture, in so far as this was possible without losing their identity. Let us ask why, then, did they struggle for several generations in sanguinary conflicts that broke out again and again with greater and greater force? A Roman writer places these words into the mouth of their leaders: "What was there left for them to do, except to maintain their liberty or perish before they became slaves?" Liberty to them meant this: persisting to remain Germans and continuing the task of settling their own problems, independently

and in consonance with the original spirit of their race
. . . , and propagating this independence in their posterity.
All the blessings which the Romans offered them, as a
result of which they would have had to become non-
German, meant slavery. They would have become half-
Roman. They assumed as a matter of course that every
German would rather die then become a Roman, and that
a true German would want to live only to be and remain
a German and to bring up his children as Germans.

They did not all perish. They did not become slaves.
They bequeathed liberty to their children. The modern
world must thank them for what it is now because of their
refusal to yield. If the Romans had succeeded in making
slaves of them, if the Romans had destroyed them as a
nation, which the Romans had done in every other case,
the entire history of the human race would have been
different. We, the inheritors of their soil, their language,
and their way of thinking, must thank them for being
Germans. . . . The other branches of the human race,
those we now regard as foreigners but who are actually
our blood-brothers, are indebted to the Germans for their
very existence. . . .

Our present problem . . . is simply to preserve the
existence and continuity of what is German. All other
differences vanish before this higher point of view. . . .
It is essential that the higher love of Fatherland, for the
entire people of the German nation, reign supreme, and
justly so, in every particular German state. No one of
them can lose sight of the higher interest without alienat-
ing everything that is noble and good. . . .

These addresses have invited you, as well as the entire
German nation, in so far as it is possible at the present
time, to rally the nation around a speaker by means of
the printed book, to come to definite decisions, and to be
of unanimous mind on the following questions:

1. Whether it is true or untrue that there exists a German nation, and whether or not its continued existence is
at the present time in danger.

2. Whether it is worthwhile, or not, to maintain this
nation.

3. Whether or not there is any certain and thorough
means of maintaining it, and what this means is.

SHELLEY'S *DECLARATION OF RIGHTS*, 1812

The literature of any given historical period accurately reflects the climate of opinion in which it appears. In most early nineteenth-century countries, poets and writers produced a mass of revolutionary, critical, and imaginative poetry and prose expressing their dissatisfaction with the political and social ills of the day. An excellent example of this literature of protest is the Declaration of Rights, *a pamphlet written by the twenty-year-old English genius, Percy Bysshe Shelley (1792-1822). At Lynmouth, Shelley's Irish servant was sentenced to six months' imprisonment, but was released in the custody of his master, for posting "the inflammatory or seditious" pamphlet. Although he was a shining light of the Romantic School, Shelley presented in his tract many of the ideas of the men of the Age of Reason. The difference was that the rationalists had based their ideas on natural law, while the youthful reformer was motivated chiefly by rebelliousness at the mere suggestion of discipline, restraint, or law, which he regarded as tyrannous.*

Shelley, crushed by the laws of the England he had ridiculed, fled his native land in March, 1818, for Italy, never to return. In 1819 he wrote a famous sonnet, the second selection below, in which he castigated the social conditions of England.

✓   ✓   ✓

A

Shelley's Declaration of Rights, *1812* [8]

1. Government has no rights; it is a delegation from several individuals for the purpose of securing their own.

[8] Percy Bysshe Shelley, *Declaration of Rights,* 1812. The broadside, printed in Ireland, bore no printer's name.

It is therefore just only so far as it exists by their consent, useful only so far as it operates to their well-being.

2. If these individuals think that the form of government which they, or their forefathers, constituted is ill adapted to produce their happiness, they have a right to change it.

3. Government is devised for the security of rights. The rights of man are liberty and an equal participation in the commonage of nature.

4. As the benefit of the governed is, or ought to be, the origin of government, no men can have any authority that does not expressly emanate from their will.

5. Though all governments are not so bad as that of Turkey, yet none are so good as they might be; the majority of every country have a right to perfect their government; the minority should not disturb them; they ought to secede and form their own system in their own way.

6. All have a right to an equal share in the benefits and burdens of government. Any disabilities for opinion imply by their existence barefaced tyranny on the side of government, ignorant slavishness on the side of the governed.

7. The rights of man in the present state of society are only to be secured by some degree of coercion to be exercised on their violator. The sufferer has a right that the degree of coercion be as slight as possible.

8. It may be considered as a plain proof of the hollowness of any proposition, if power be used to enforce instead of reason to persuade its admission. Government is never supported by fraud until it cannot be supported by reason.

9. No man has a right to disturb the public peace by personally resisting the execution of a law however bad. He ought to acquiesce, using at the same time the utmost powers of his reason to promote its repeal.

10. A man must have a right to act in a certain manner before it can be his duty. He may, before he ought.

11. A man has a right to think as his reason directs; it is a duty he owes to himself to think with freedom, that he may act from conviction.

12. A man has a right to unrestricted liberty of dis-

cussion; falsehood is a scorpion that will sting itself to death.

13. A man has not only a right to express his thoughts, but it is his duty to do so.

14. No law has a right to discourage the practice of truth. A man ought to speak the truth on every occasion; a duty can never be criminal; what is not criminal cannot be injurious.

15. Law cannot make what is in its nature virtuous or innocent to be criminal, any more than it can make what is criminal to be innocent. Government cannot make a law; it can only pronounce that which was the law before its organization—viz., the moral result of the imperishable relations of things.

16. The present generation cannot bind their posterity. The few cannot promise for the many.

17. No man has a right to do an evil thing that good may come.

18. Expediency is inadmissible in morals. Politics are only sound when conducted on principles of morality. They are, in fact, the morals of nations.

19. Man has no right to kill his brother; it is no excuse that he does so in uniform. He only adds the infamy of servitude to the crime of murder.

20. Man, whatever be his country, has the same rights in one place as another, the rights of universal citizenship.

21. The government of a country ought to be perfectly indifferent to every opinion. Religious differences, the bloodiest and most rancorous of all, spring from partiality.

22. A delegation of individuals, for the purpose of securing their rights, can have no undelegated power of restraining the expression of their opinion.

23. Belief is involuntary; nothing involuntary is meritorious or reprehensible. A man ought not to be considered worse or better for his belief.

24. A Christian, a Deist, a Turk, and a Jew have equal rights: they are men and brethren.

25. If a person's religious ideas correspond not with your own, love him nevertheless. How different would yours have been, had the chance of birth placed you in Tartary or India!

26. Those who believe that Heaven is, what earth has

been, a monopoly in the hands of a favored few, would do well to reconsider their opinion: if they find that it came from their priest or their grandmother, they could not do better than reject it.

27. No man has a right to be respected for any other possessions but those of virtue and talent. Titles are tinsel, power a corruptor, glory a bubble, and excessive wealth a libel on its possessor.

28. No man has a right to monopolize more than he can enjoy; what the rich give to the poor, whilst millions are starving, is not a perfect favor, but an imperfect right.

29. Every man has a right to a certain degree of leisure and liberty, because it is his duty to attain a certain degree of knowledge. He may, before he ought.

30. Sobriety of body and mind is necessary to those who would be free, because without sobriety a high sense of philanthropy cannot actuate the heart, nor cool and determined courage execute its dictates.

31. The only use of government is to repress the vices of man. If man were today, sinless, tomorrow he would have a right to demand that government and all its evils should cease.

Man! thou whose rights are here declared, be no longer forgetful of the loftiness of thy destination. Think of thy rights; of those possessions which will give thee virtue and wisdom, by which thou mayest arrive at happiness and freedom. They are declared to thee by one who knows thy dignity, for every hour does his heart swell with honorable pride in the contemplation of what thou mayest attain, by one who is not forgetful of thy degeneracy, for every moment brings home to him the bitter conviction of what thou art.

Awake!—arise!—or be forever fallen.

B

Shelley's Sonnet: England in 1819 [9]

An old, mad, blind, despised, and dying king,—[10]

---

[9] Percy Bysshe Shelley, *Poetical Works* (London, 1890), p. 524.

[10] George III, King of England (1760-1820), who became hopelessly insane in 1810.

Princes, the dregs of their dull race, who flow
Through public scorn,—mud from a muddy spring,—
Rulers who neither see, nor feel, nor know,
But leech-like to their fainting country cling,
Till they drop, blind in blood, without a blow,—
A people starved and stabbed in the untilled field,—
An army, which liberticide and prey
Makes as a two-edged sword to all who wield,—
Golden and sanguine laws which tempt and slay;
Religion, Christless, Godless—a book sealed;
A Senate,—Time's worst statute unrepealed,—[11]
Are graves, from which a glorious Phantom[12] may
Burst, to illumine our tempestuous day.

— 7 —

ABDICATION OF NAPOLEON
APRIL 11, 1814

Napoleon understood the meaning of his own life when he said in St. Helena: "Centuries will pass before the unique combination of events which led to my career recur in the case of another." France had fallen into political and social confusion after the collapse of the Old Régime. At precisely the critical moment, Napoleon appeared, rose to supreme power, gave France two decades of glory, and then left her with the humiliation of a decisive defeat. To some, he was a source of inspiration, a

[11] Shelley here refers to the laws restricting the liberties of Roman Catholics. It was repealed in the Emancipation Act of 1829.
[12] The word "Phantom" refers to "liberty."

superman who had brought honor and prestige to France, while to others he was a vile, bloodthirsty creature, who represented human barbarism at its lowest point. Somewhere between these estimates appears the figure of one of the great military geniuses of history, whose amazing aptitude in war was matched by a remarkable skill in the art of government. Ironically, the same man who rejected all moral considerations in his conduct, and could dismiss the loss of a thousand fanatically loyal soldiers as trivial, was able to consolidate many of the gains of the French Revolution.

It took a powerful European coalition to strike down the "Corsican Ogre." His fiercest critics, the English, greeted his abdication with this verse:

Boney, canker of our joys, now thy Tyrant reign is o'er,
Fill the merry bowl, my boys, join in bacchanalian roar;
Seize the villain, plunge him in, see the hated miscreant dies.
Mirth and all thy train come in; banish sorrows, tears, and sighs.

✓   ✓   ✓

A

First Abdication of Napoleon, April 4, 1814 [13]

The Allied Powers, having proclaimed that the Emperor Napoleon has been the only obstacle to the reestablishment of peace in Europe, the Emperor Napoleon, loyal to his oath, hereby declares that he is prepared to descend from the throne and even to give his life for the welfare of the fatherland. This, however, cannot be regarded as separated from the rights of his son, those of the regency of the Empress, and the laws of the Empire.

Done at our palace of Fontainebleu, April 4, 1814.

NAPOLEON

[13] Faustin Adolphe Hélie, *Les constitutions de la France* (Paris, 1880), p. 878.

B

Second Abdication of Napoleon, April 11, 1814 [14]

The Allied Powers, having proclaimed that the Emperor Napoleon has been the only obstacle to the reestablishment of peace in Europe, the Emperor Napoleon, loyal to his oath, hereby declares that he renounces, for himself, and for his heirs, the thrones of France and Italy. Furthermore, there is no personal sacrifice, even that of life, which he would not make for France.

Done at the palace of Fontainebleu, April 11, 1814.

— 8 —

THE FRENCH CONSTITUTIONAL CHARTER OF JUNE 4, 1814 [15]

Following the overthrow of Napoleon, the Allied powers agreed to the restoration of the Bourbons in France provided that constitutional guarantees were given to the French people. The famous Constitutional Charter of 1814 represented a compromise between the rights of the people and the rights of the monarchy. It reflected the important gains of the French Revolution, showing especially the influence of the cahiers, and, at the same time, stated the limits of what the restored Bourbons would accept.

[14] A.J.H. and Jules de Clercq, *Receuil des traités de la France, publié sous les auspices du ministère des affaires étrangères* (Paris, 1864-1917), II, 402.

[15] Duvergier, J. B., *et al.*, *Collection complète des lois, décrets, ordonnances, règlements, avis du Conseil d'État*, 2nd ed., 31 vols. (Paris, 1838-   ), XIX, 59 ff.

A

Public Rights of the French

1. Frenchmen are equal before the law, whatever their titles or ranks.

2. They contribute without distinction in ratio to their fortunes, to the expenses of the State.

3. They are all equally admissible to civil and military employment.

4. Their personal liberty is likewise guaranteed. No one can be prosecuted nor arrested except in cases provided by the law and in the form prescribed.

5. Every person may profess his religion with equal liberty, and shall enjoy the same protection.

6. However, the Catholic Apostolic and Roman religion is declared to be the religion of the State.

7. The ministers of the Catholic Apostolic and Roman religion and those of other Christian sects shall alone receive stipends from the Royal Treasury.

8. Frenchmen have the right to publish and print their opinions, provided that these opinions conform with the laws necessary to restrain abuses of that liberty.

9. All property is inviolable, even that of property which is called *national*. The law makes no distinction between the two.

10. The State can require the sacrifice of property in the cause of public interest, provided that previous indemnity has been made.

11. All investigation of opinion and votes given before the Restoration is forbidden. The same prohibition is required for tribunals and for citizens.

12. Conscription is abolished. The method of recruiting for the army and navy is determined by law.

B

Form of Government of the King

13. The person of the King is sacred and inviolable. His ministers are responsible. The executive power is vested only in the King.

14. The King is the supreme head of the State. He has command of the land and naval forces; he declares war; he concludes treaties of peace, alliance, and commerce; he appoints all the officials of the public administration; and he issues the regulations and decrees necessary for the execution of the laws and the safety of the State.

15. Legislative power is exercised jointly by the King, the Chamber of Peers, and the Chamber of Deputies of the Departments.

16. The King has the right of initiating legislation.

17. Proposed legislation is submitted, at the choice of the King, either to the Chamber of Peers or to the Chamber of Deputies, with the exception of tax laws, which must be submitted to the Chamber of Deputies.

18. Every law must be discussed and passed freely by a majority of both houses.

19. The Chambers possess the right to petition the King to submit legislation relating to any subject and to suggest what they feel the legislation should contain. . . .

[*There follow 49 articles defining the powers of the Chamber of Peers, the Chamber of Deputies of the Departments, the Ministers, and the Judiciary.*]

C

Special Rights Guaranteed by the State

69. Persons in active military service, retired officers and soldiers, pensioned widows, and officers and soldiers retain their ranks, commissions, and pensions.

70. The public debt is guaranteed. Every form of engagement made by the State with its creditors is inviolable.

71. The old nobility resume their titles. The new attain their titles. The King may make nobles at will, but he grants to them only ranks and honors without an exemption for the burdens and duties of society.

72. The Legion of Honor is maintained. The King shall determine its external regulations and its decoration.

73. The colonies shall be governed by special laws and regulations.

74. The King and his successors shall swear, at the

ceremony of their coronation, to observe faithfully the present Constitutional Charter. . . .

Given at Paris, in the year of grace, 1814, and of our reign the nineteenth.

(Signed) LOUIS [XVIII]

— 9 —

THE GERMAN CONFEDERATION, JUNE 8, 1815 [16]

Many temporal and ecclesiastical princes of the more than three hundred pre-Revolutionary German states (as well as some of the fifteen hundred Imperial Knights) converged on Vienna in 1815 to demand their restoration on the principle of "legitimacy." But the statesmen of Vienna made no attempt to revive the Holy Roman Empire which Napoleon had dissolved in 1806. The larger states, as Austria, Prussia, Bavaria, and Württemberg, which had suppressed their smaller neighbors, were in no mood to diminish their own power.

Instead of the Holy Roman Empire, there was now organized the German Confederation, consisting of thirty-eight states, thus leaving the Napoleonic solution of the German question virtually undisturbed. The German Act of Confederation, from which excerpts are given below, reflected the rivalry of Austria and Prussia. Germany remained essentially a "geographical expression," bound together only by an impotent Diet. This constitution, which established a loose union of sovereign princes, remained in force from 1815 to 1866, when Austrian domination was finally and successfully challenged by Prussia.

[16] P. A. G. von Meyer, *Corpus juris confoederationis Germanicae*, 2nd ed. (Frankfurt am Main, 1833), II, 3 ff.

*Extracts from the German Act of Confederation,
June 8, 1815*

In the name of the Most Holy and Indivisible Trinity:

The sovereign princes and the free towns of Germany, motivated by their common desire to implement Article VI of the Peace of Paris (May 30, 1814), and convinced of the advantages which would accrue for the security and independence of Germany and for the well-being and equilibrium of Europe from a strong and lasting union, have agreed to unite themselves in a perpetual confederation, and, for this reason, have given their representatives and envoys at the Congress of Vienna full powers. . . .

ARTICLE 1. The sovereign princes and the free towns of Germany, including their Majesties, the Emperor of Austria and the Kings of Prussia, Denmark, and the Netherlands—the Emperor of Austria and the King of Prussia because of their possessions formerly belonging to the German Empire; the King of Denmark for Holstein; and the King of the Netherlands for the Grand Duchy of Luxemburg—unite in a perpetual union which shall be called the German Confederation.

ARTICLE 2. The aim of this Confederation shall be the maintenance of the external and internal security of Germany as well as the independence and inviolability of the individual German States.

ARTICLE 3. All members of the Confederation shall have equal rights. They all agree to maintain the Act of Confederation.

ARTICLE 4. The affairs of the Confederation shall be managed by a Diet of the Confederation, in which all members of the Confederation shall vote through their representatives, either individually or collectively, in the following manner, without prejudice to their rank:

	Votes			Votes
1. Austria	1	6. Württemberg	. .	1
2. Prussia	1	7. Baden	. .	1
3. Bavaria	1	8. Electoral Hesse	.	1
4. Saxony	1	9. Grand duchy of		
5. Hanover	1	Hesse	. .	1

	VOTES
10. Denmark, for Holstein	1
11. The Netherlands, for the grand duchy of Luxemburg	1
12. The grand ducal and ducal houses of Saxony	1
13. Brunswick and Nassau	1
14. Mecklenburg-Schwerin and Mecklenburg-Strelitz	1
15. Holstein-Oldenburg, Anhalt, and Schwarzburg	1
16. Hohenzollern, Liechtenstein, Reuss, Schaumburg-Lippe, Lippe, and Waldeck	1
17. The free towns, Lübeck, Frankfurt, Bremen, and Hamburg	1
Total votes	17

ARTICLE 5. Austria shall preside over the Diet of the Confederation. Each member of the Confederation shall have the right to initiate and support proposals. Austria as the presiding state is bound within a given period to bring these proposals to deliberation.

ARTICLE 6. When fundamental laws of the Confederation are to be enacted or amended . . . the Diet shall exist as a general assembly, in which the distribution of the votes, based upon the geographical extent of the individual states, shall be as follows:

	VOTES
1. Austria	4
2. Prussia	4
3. Saxony	4
4. Bavaria	4
5. Hanover	4
6. Württemberg	4
7. Baden	3
8. Electoral Hesse	3
9. Grand duchy of Hesse	3
10. Holstein	3
11. Luxemburg	3
12. Brunswick	2
13. Mecklenburg-Schwerin	2
14. Nassau	2
15. Saxe-Weimar	1
16. Saxe-Gotha	1
17. Saxe-Coburg	1
18. Saxe-Meiningen	1
19. Saxe-Hildburghausen	1
20. Mecklenburg-Strelitz	1
21. Holstein-Oldenburg	1
22. Anhalt-Dessau	1
23. Anhalt-Bernburg	1
24. Anhalt-Cöthen	1
25. Schwarzburg-Sondershausen	1

	Votes		Votes
26. Schwarzburg-Rudol-stadt	1	33. Schaumberg-Lippe	1
27. Hohenzollern-Hechingen	1	34. Lippe	1
28. Liechtenstein	1	35. The Free Town Lübeck	1
29. Hohenzollern-Sig-maringen	1	36. The Free Town Frankfurt	1
30. Waldeck	1	37. The Free Town Bremen	1
31. Reuss, Elder Branch	1	38. The Free Town Hamburg	1
32. Reuss, Younger Branch	1		
Total votes			69

ARTICLE 9. The Diet of the Confederation shall meet at Frankfurt am Main. The first meeting shall take place on September 1, 1815. . . .

ARTICLE 11. All members of the Confederation pledge themselves to protect Germany as a whole, and also every single confederated state, against attack. . . . If war is declared by the Confederation, no individual member may negotiate separately with the enemy, conclude an armistice, or make peace.

ARTICLE 12. The members of the Confederation reserve to themselves the right of forming alliances of any kind. However, they pledge themselves to make no commitments that shall be directed against the security of the Confederation or any individual state within it.

THE HOLY ALLIANCE, SEPTEMBER 14-26, 1815 [17]

After the defeat of Napoleon at Waterloo, Great Britain, Russia, Austria, and Prussia were motivated by one commanding thought—to prevent France from rising again as a disturber of the peace of Europe. For a quarter of a century these countries had made war on the French Republic and the French Empire. Tsar Alexander I, whose character was tinged with mysticism, saw in the downfall of Napoleon the work of Providence. Accordingly, he requested his fellow sovereigns to sign a document guaranteeing that, henceforth, the relations between nations would be based on "the sublime truths of the Holy Religion." Frederick William III, King of Prussia, and Francis I, Emperor of Austria, subscribed to the pact, which was formally signed on September 26, 1815.

1   1   1

In the name of the Most Holy and Indivisible Trinity.

Their Majesties, the Emperor of Austria, the King of Prussia, and the Emperor of Russia, having, in consequence of the great events which have marked the course of the last three years in Europe, and especially of the blessings which it has pleased Divine Providence to shower down upon those States which place their confidence and their hope on it alone, acquired the intimate conviction of the necessity of settling the steps to be observed by the Powers, in their reciprocal relations, upon the sublime truths which the Holy Religion of our Saviour teaches;

They solemnly declare that the present Act has no other object than to publish, in the face of the whole

---

[17] E. Hertslet, ed., *The Map of Europe by Treaty* (London, 1875), I, 317-19.

world, their fixed resolution, both in the administration of their respective States, and in their political relations with every other Government, to take for their sole guide the precepts of that Holy Religion, namely, the precepts of Justice, Christian Charity, and Peace, which, far from being applicable only to private concerns, must have an immediate influence on the council of Princes, and guide all their steps, as being the only means of consolidating human institutions and remedying their imperfections. In consequence, their Majesties have agreed upon the following Articles:—

ARTICLE 1. Conformably to the words of the Holy Scriptures, which command all men to consider each other as brethren, the three contracting Monarchs will remain united by the bonds of a true and indissoluble fraternity, and considering each other as fellow countrymen, they will, on all occasions and in all places, lend each other aid and assistance; and, regarding themselves towards their subjects and armies as fathers of families, they will lead them, in the same spirit of fraternity with which they are animated, to protect Religion, Peace, and Justice.

ARTICLE 2. In consequence, the sole principle of force, whether between the said Governments or between their subjects, shall be that of doing each other reciprocal service, and of testifying by unalterable good will the mutual affection with which they ought to be animated, to consider themselves all as members of one and the same Christian nation; the three allied Princes looking on themselves as merely delegated by Providence to govern three branches of the One family, namely, Austria, Prussia, and Russia, thus confessing that the Christian world, of which they and their people form a part, has in reality no other Sovereign than Him to whom alone power really belongs, because in Him alone are found the treasures of love, science, and infinite wisdom, that is to say, God, our Divine Saviour, the Word of the Most High, the Word of Life. Their Majesties consequently recommend to their people, with the most tender solicitude, as the sole means of enjoying that Peace which arises from a good conscience, and which alone is durable, to strengthen themselves every day more and more in the

principles and exercise of the duties which the Divine
Saviour has taught to mankind.

ARTICLE 3. All the Powers who shall choose solemnly to avow the sacred principles which have dictated
the present Act, and shall acknowledge how important it
is for the happiness of nations, too long agitated, that these
truths should henceforth exercise over the destinies of
mankind all the influence which belongs to them, will be
received with equal ardour and affection into this Holy
Alliance.

Done in triplicate, and signed at Paris, the year of
Grace 1815, 14-26 September.

(L.S.) FRANCIS
(L.S.) FREDERICK WILLIAM
(L.S.) ALEXANDER

— 11 —

THE QUADRUPLE ALLIANCE, NOVEMBER 20, 1815 [18]

*The Holy Alliance was promptly confused in the popu-
lar mind with the Quadruple Alliance. Where the former
was a vague declaration of principles, the Quadruple Alliance was a definite treaty concluded for practical ends.
When the Second Peace of Paris was concluded, the four
Great Powers—Great Britain, Russia, Prussia, and Austria—signed a pact at Paris on November 20, 1815 formally confirming the earlier agreements. The alliance agreed
to maintain by force the settlement made at the Congress
of Vienna, to meet at stated intervals to discuss matters of*

[18] E. Hertslet, ed., *The Map of Europe by Treaty* (London,
1875), I, 372-77.

common interest, and to guarantee the peace of Europe. While at first ostensibly directed at France alone, the alliance soon became an instrument dedicated to the preservation of the status quo *against liberal and democratic movements. In effect, it meant the organization of reaction.*

✔   ✔   ✔

In the name of the most Holy and Undivided Trinity.

The purpose of the alliance concluded at Vienna the 25th day of March, 1815, having been happily attained by the re-establishment in France of the order of things which the last criminal attempt of Napoleon Bonaparte had momentarily subverted; their Majesties the King of the United Kingdom of Great Britain and Ireland, the Emperor of Austria, King of Hungary and Bohemia, the Emperor of all the Russians, and the King of Prussia, considering that the repose of Europe is essentially interwoven with the confirmation of the order of things founded on the maintenance of the royal authority and of the constitutional charter, and wishing to employ all their means to prevent the general tranquillity (the object of the wishes of mankind and the constant end of their efforts), from being again disturbed, desirous, moreover, to draw closer the ties which unite them for the common interests of their people, have resolved to give to the principles solemnly laid down in the treaties of Chaumont on the 1st March, 1814, and of Vienna of the 25th of March, 1815, the application the most analogous to the present state of affairs, and to fix beforehand by a solemn treaty the principles which they propose to follow, in order to guarantee Europe from dangers by which she may still be menaced; for which purpose the high contracting parties have named to discuss, settle, and sign the conditions of this treaty, namely: . . .

ARTICLE 1. The high contracting parties reciprocally promise to maintain, in its force and vigor, the treaty signed this day with his most Christian Majesty, and to see that the stipulations of the said treaty, as well as those of the particular conventions which have reference thereto shall be strictly and faithfully executed in their fullest extent.

ARTICLE 2. The high contracting parties, having engaged in the war which has just terminated, for the purpose of maintaining inviolably the arrangements settled at Paris last year for the safety and interest of Europe, have judged it advisable to renew the said engagements by the present act, and to confirm them as mutually obligatory, subject to the modifications contained in the treaty signed this day with the plenipotentiaries of his most Christian Majesty, and particularly those by which Napoleon Bonaparte and his family, in pursuance of the treaty of the 11th of April, 1814, have been forever excluded from supreme power in France, which exclusion the contracting powers bind themselves by the present act to maintain in full vigor, and, should it be necessary, with the whole of their forces. And as the same revolutionary principles which upheld the last criminal usurpation, might again, under other forms, convulse France, and thereby endanger the repose of other states; under these circumstances, the high contracting parties solemnly admitting it to be their duty to redouble their watchfulness for the tranquillity and interests of their people, engage, in case so unfortunate an event should again occur, to concert amongst themselves, and with His Most Christian Majesty, the measures which they may judge necessary to be pursued for the safety of their respective states, and for the general tranquillity of Europe. . . .

ARTICLE 5. The high contracting parties having agreed to the dispositions laid down in the preceding articles, for the purpose of securing the effect of their engagements during the period of the temporary occupation, declare, moreover, that even after the expiration of this measure, the said engagements shall still remain in full force and vigor, for the purpose of carrying into effect such measures as may be deemed necessary for the maintenance of the stipulations contained in Articles 1 and 2 of the present act.

ARTICLE 6. To facilitate and to secure the execution of the present treaty, and to consolidate the connections which at the present moment so closely unite the four sovereigns for the happiness of the world, the high contracting parties have agreed to renew their meetings at fixed periods, either under the immediate auspices of the sovereigns themselves, or by their respective ministers, for the purpose of consulting upon their common interests, and for the consideration of the measures which at each of those periods shall be considered the most salutary for the repose and prosperity of nations, and for the maintenance of the peace of Europe.

ARTICLE 7. The present treaty shall be ratified, and the ratifications shall be exchanged within two months, or sooner, if possible.

In faith of which the respective plenipotentiaries have signed it, and affixed thereto the seal of their arms.

Done at Paris, the 20th of November, in the year of our Lord, 1815.

(L.S.) CASTLEREAGH   (L.S.) METTERNICH
(L.S.) WELLINGTON   (L.S.) WESSENBERG

— 12 —

THE ITALIAN *CARBONARI,* 1817-24

The Carbonari ("charcoal-burners") played an important role in the Italian Risorgimento (Resurrection). Organized in the latter days of the Napoleonic Empire and carried over after 1815 into the period of Austrian domination, the society aimed at freeing the country from foreign rule and obtaining constitutional liberties. It comprised army officers, nobles, landlords, government officials, workers, peasants, and even priests. The movement spread through southern Italy. Among the foreigners who joined it were Lord Byron, and Louis Napoleon was implicated in it in his early years.

The Carbonari used Christian and liberal phraseology in their constitutions: "Carbonarism teaches the true end of moral existence, and gives rules of conduct for social life. . . . It is to the sacred rights of equality that the Good Cousins (buoni cugini) *must especially attach themselves." Their fantastic symbolism, esoteric and mysterious, was designed to appeal to the uneducated masses. The members used a secret and impenetrable correspondence, by means of a dictionary of various words, referable to others of real meaning.*

Harried by the Austrian police, the Carbonari, nevertheless, took a leading part in the revolutions of 1820 and 1830. Many members were executed, imprisoned, or exiled. The movement gradually faded away; its place was taken by Mazzini's Young Italy Society. But the Carbonari helped prepare the way for the expulsion of Austria from Italian affairs and for the unification of Italy.

⌁   ⌁   ⌁

A

Proclamation of the Carbonari, *June 24, 1817* [19]

People of the Roman States (*Popoli Pontifici*)!

When it is the will of the Most High God to punish nations, He consigns them to the government of idiots.

When He sees that they are sensible of their errors and wills their happiness, he inspires them with courage and commands them to shake off the yoke of oppression (*il bargaro gingo*).

People of the Roman States! You have already suffered long enough—the scythe of Pestilence and Famine will complete your destruction and that of our children, if you delay any longer to protect yourselves.

To arms, then! to arms! Let your battle-word be the love of your country and compassion (*carità*) for your offspring.

To overthrow the despot, to tax the rich and to succour the indigent are your sole objects. You have only to show yourselves resolutely (*col vostro aspetto imponente*) and order and justice will triumph.

History already prepares for you a distinguished rank among her heroes.

[19] *Memoirs of the Secret Societies of the South of Italy, Particularly the Carbonari,* translated from the original (London, 1821), p. 186.

People, to arms!

He alone is worthy of life (*viva solo chi*) who loves his country and succours the wretched. The people of the Marches and of Romagna are devoted to our cause. Last evening they embraced it, and are you, blind people, asleep?

B

Oaths and Symbols of the Carbonari, 1817 [20]

1. The First Rank; the Apprentice Carbonaro

The Sworn Oath: I, N.N., promise and swear, upon the general statutes of the order, and upon this steel, the avenging instrument of the perjured, scrupulously to keep the secret of Carbonarism, and neither to write, engrave, or paint anything concerning it, without having obtained a written permission. I swear to help my Good Cousins in care and need, as much as in me lies, and not to attempt anything against the honor of their families. I consent, and wish, if I perjure myself, that my body may be cut in pieces, then burnt, and my ashes scattered to the wind, in order that my name may be held up to the execration of the Good Cousins throughout the earth. So help me God!"

Password: The apprentices have none.

Sacred Words: Fede, Speranza, Carità (Faith, Hope, Charity), pronounced in spelling.

Touch: Ͼ_____ •• (These signs and touches are made with the middle finger on the right thumb of the fellow-apprentice.)

Decorations: Three ribbons—black, blue, and red, with the specimen of wood.

2. The Second Rank: the Master Carbonaro

The Sworn Oath: I, N.N., promise and swear before the Grand Master of the Universe, upon my word and honor, and upon this steel, the avenging instrument of the

[20] *Ibid.,* pp. 196, 201-03, 32-33. These oaths and symbols were used by the Supreme Lodge, or *Alta Vendita,* at Naples, in 1817. They became part of the court record at a trial of the members.

perjured, to keep scrupulously and inviolably the secrets of Carbonarism, never to talk of those of the Apprentices before the Pagans, nor of those of the Masters before the Apprentices. As also, not to initiate any person, nor to establish a Vendita without permission and in a just and perfect number—not to write or engrave the secrets—to help even with my blood, if necessary, the Good Cousins Carbonari, and to attempt nothing against the honor of their families. I consent, if I perjure myself, to have my body cut in pieces, then burnt, and the ashes scattered to the wind, that my name may remain in execration and with all Good Cousins Carbonari spread over the face of the earth. So help me God!

Password: Felce, Ortica (Fern, Nettle).

Sacred Words: Onore, Virtù, Probità (Honor, Virtue, Integrity), pronounced in spelling.

Touch: ⊕ • _____ •• _____ •• (These signs and touches are made with the middle finger on the right thumb of the fellow-master.)

Decorations: The specimen of silver, with a tricolored scarf—black, blue, and red.

3. Meaning of the Symbols of the Carbonari, Macerata, 1817

[*In the Neapolitan Constitution of the Carbonari at Macerata the various symobls of the society were given innocuous definitions. For example, the symbol of a ladder was explained this way:* "[The ladder shows that] *virtue is only to be obtained step by step.*" *However, the minutes of the trial of an accused group of members reveal that all the symbols had secondary meanings known only to the Carbonari. Following are these secret meanings. Note the definition of "ladder":*]

1. *Cross:* To crucify the tyrant.
2. *Crown of Thorns:* To pierce his head.
3. *Thread:* The cord to lead him to the gibbet.
4. *Ladder:* To aid the tyrant to mount the gibbet.
5. *Leaves:* Nails to pierce his hands and feet.
6. *Pick-axe:* To penetrate his breast.
7. *Axe:* To separate his head from his body.
8. *Salt:* To prevent the corruption of his head, that it may last as a monument of the eternal infamy of despots.

9. *Pole:* To mount the skull of the tyrant.

10. *Furnace:* To burn his body.

11. *Shovel:* To scatter his ashes to the wind.

12. *Baracca:* To prepare new tortures for the tyrant.

13. *Fountain:* To purify us from the vile blood we shall have shed.

14. *Linen:* To wipe away our stains and render us clean and pure.

15. *Forest:* Place where the Good Cousins labor to obtain so important a result.

C

Contemporary Accounts of the Carbonari, *1820-24* [21]

1. Origins

The passion for a representative government had long existed in the south of Italy, amid the better and middling classes of society. The secret associations, known by the name of Carbonari (of which as yet we know little with certainty, except their existence and their name), preserved and diffused this passion and afforded it the means of displaying itself in action. And such was the influence of the Carbonari, even as far back as 1814, that, in that year, 15 Neapolitan generals formed a plan, which accidents afterwards induced them to lay aside, of marching upon Naples with 12,000 men, who were cantoned in the marshes, in order to force Murat to grant a constitution.

2. The Carbonari in Florence, the Romagna, and Lombardy, 1821

After the breaking out of the revolution in Piedmont, a plot was said to have been discovered for effecting a similar change in Florence. It embraced only a few individuals of no great consequence to the state. Some officers of the army, none of them above the rank of Captain, were, on suspicion of being engaged in it, first put under arrest, then dismissed from the service, and subsequently ordered to leave the country. One of them,

[21] These eyewitness accounts are taken from the *Annual Register, 1820,* p. 238; *1822,* p. 244; and *1824,* pp. 194-95.

a Captain Baldine, when under arrest in his own house, threw himself out of the window, and was killed on the spot. Among the persons accused of being Carbonari, or of being engaged in the confederacy, was a priest, a man of considerable talent and eloquence, famous for the crowds which he attracted by his lectures, in the church of Santa Croce. . . .

In Romagna, many persons were arrested as Carbonari, and a still greater number of them in Lombardy. Thirty-four of them were brought to trial. [*Most*] were punished with a few months imprisonment for transgressing the police regulations; the remainder were condemned to death as guilty of high treason: but this sentence was afterwards commuted into imprisonment, in the castle at Spielberg, for 21 years, in three of the cases, and for 10 years in the rest.

3. Imprisonment in the Fortress of Spielberg, 1824

Two years had elapsed since Count Frederick Gonfalonieri, Pallavicini, and many other Italians of high rank had been imprisoned by the Austrian authorities, on a charge of being leaders in the supposed conspiracy of the Carbonari; and, during this period, nothing with respect to their fate was known.

At length, in January, 1824, it was announced to the world, that Gonfalonieri, and seven others, who were in custody, were condemned to death as guilty of high treason, and that several more, who had found safety in flight, were condemned, as contumacious, to the same doom.

The proceedings were in secret, before a special commission of Austrian judges; so that there are no means of knowing the nature of the facts proved, nor the quality of the evidence. But the alleged criminals do not appear to have been such as the accused we are ashamed of.

"Gonfalonieri," said the Austrian demi-official account of the proceedings, "far from manifesting the smallest repentance in the whole course of the proceedings, constantly displayed the most invincible obstinacy in his crime, of which he made a complete confession with a sort of boasting."

An imperial decree, which accompanied the promulgation of the sentence, commuted it in favor of those who were in custody, to imprisonment of the severest character (*carcere duro*) in the fortress of Spielberg in Moravia. There these unfortunate men were doomed to pass the remainder of their lives, clothed in prison dresses of the coarsest cloth, sleeping upon the ground, with the blackest bread and water for their daily food, and excluded from all intercourse with each other, or with any friend or relation. Their sentence was to be read to them once every year, and, at each sad anniversary they were to be severely beaten with sticks. The absent were executed in effigy; Gonfalonieri and the rest of the prisoners were exposed on the public scaffold, bound hand and foot in chains, with the executioner at their side; and in this situation, the imperial decree for sparing their lives was read to them.

— 13 —

THE CARLSBAD DECREES, SEPTEMBER 1, 1819[22]

The basic principle of Metternich's policy was to maintain the German Confederation under Austrian domination. He strongly opposed any efforts at German national unification, for fear that the diverse elements within Austria's borders might catch the fever of nationalism and demand independence. Thoroughly annoyed by the dangerous Wartburg Festival, he was goaded into more repressive action when, on March 23, 1819, a fanatical student named Karl Sand murdered Kotzebue,

[22] P. A. G. von Meyer, *Corpus juris confoederationis Germanicae* 2nd ed. (Frankfurt am Main, 1833), II, 138 ff.

a reactionary journalist suspected of being a spy in the pay of the Russian tsar.

In response to this murder (Sand was publicly executed for it) and other attempted assassinations, Metternich drew up the Carlsbad Decrees, which provided for special officials in the German universities to supervise the conduct of students and teachers, established a rigid censorship, and called for the arrest and imprisonment of vociferous German patriots. The decrees, subsequently confirmed by the Federal Diet at Frankfurt, suppressed liberty in the Germanies for a full generation, and, in effect, determined what kind of political system the Germanies were to have for the time being.

✓   ✓   ✓

1. There shall be appointed for each university a special representative of the ruler of each State, the said representatives to have appropriate instructions and extended powers, and they shall have their place of residence where the university is located. This office may be held by the current rector or by any other individual whom the Government considers to be qualified.

This representative shall enforce strictly the existing laws and disciplinary regulations; he shall observe with care the attitude shown by the university instructors in their public lectures and registered courses; and he shall, without directly interfering in scientific matters or in teaching methods, give a beneficial direction to the teaching, keeping in view the future attitude of the students. Finally, he shall give unceasing attention to everything that may promote morality . . . among the students. . . .

2. The confederated governments mutually pledge themselves to eliminate from the universities or any other public educational institutions all instructors who shall have obviously proven their unfitness for the important work entrusted to them by openly deviating from their duties, or by going beyond the boundaries of their functions, or by abusing their legitimate influence over young minds, or by presenting harmful ideas hostile to public order or subverting existing governmental instructions. . . .

Any instructor who has been removed in this manner becomes ineligible for a position in any other public institution of learning in another state of the Confederation.

3. The laws that for some time have been directed against secret and unauthorized societies in the universities shall be strictly enforced. Such laws are applicable especially to the association formed some years ago under the name of *Allgemeine Burschenschaft,* for the organization of that society implies the completely impermissible idea of permanent fellowship and constant intercommunication between the universities. The special representatives of the Government are enjoined to exert great care in watching these organizations.

The governments mutually agree that all individuals who shall be shown to have maintained their membership in secret or unauthorized associations, or shall have taken membership in such associations, shall not be eligible for any public office.

4. No student who shall have been expelled from any university by virtue of a decision of the University Senate ratified or initiated by the special representative of the Government, shall be admitted by any other university. . . .

1. As long as this edict remains in force, no publication which appears daily, or as a serial not exceeding twenty sheets of printed matter, shall be printed in any State of the Confederation without the prior knowledge and approval of the State officials. . . .

4. Each State of the Confederation is responsible, not only to the State against which the offense is directly committed, but to the entire Confederation, for any publication printed within the limits of its judisdiction, in which the honor or security of other States is impinged upon or their constitution or administration attacked. . . .

7. When a newspaper or periodical is suppressed by a decision of the Diet, the editor of such publication may not within five years edit a similar publication in any State of the Confederation.

THE MONROE DOCTRINE, DECEMBER 2, 1823[23]

The Monroe Doctrine, the fundamental principle of the foreign policy of the United States concerning its attitude toward the interference of non-American powers in American affairs, was laid down in a series of documents by President James Monroe (1758-1831) between the years 1817 and 1823. It contained these major points: (1) American territorial integrity would be preserved against European acquisitions; (2) the political system in the Americas is essentially different from that of Europe; (3) the destinies of the Latin-American republics must not be controlled by European powers; and (4) the United States would not interfere with existing colonies or dependencies of European powers in the New World. The Monroe Doctrine received little attention at the time of its announcement, but it became of major significance after the middle of the nineteenth century. There were several cases in which its silent influence prevented intervention. The following extract from President Monroe's seventh annual message to Congress on December 2, 1823 contains the best statement of the main points of the doctrine.

✓   ✓   ✓

. . . At the proposal of the Russian Imperial Government, made through the minister of the Emperor residing here, a full power and instructions have been transmitted to the minister of the United States at St. Petersburg to arrange by amicable negotiations the re-

[23] From President James Monroe's address to Congress, August 7, 1823. Quoted in James D. Richardson, ed., *Compilation of the Messages and Papers of the Presidents, 1789-1897* (Washington, 1896-99), II, 207 ff.

spective rights and interests of the two nations on the
northwest coast of this continent. A similar proposal
has been made by His Imperial Majesty to the Government of Great Britain, which has likewise been acceded
to. The Government of the United States has been desirous by this friendly proceeding of manifesting the
great value which they have invariably attached to the
friendship of the Emperor and their solicitude to cultivate the best understanding with his Government. In
the discussion to which this interest has given rise and
in the arrangements by which they may terminate the
occasion has been judged proper for asserting, as a
principle in which the rights and interests of the United
States are involved, that the American continents, by
the free and independent condition which they have assumed and maintain, are henceforth not to be considered
as subjects for future colonization by any European
powers. . . .

It was stated at the commencement of the last session
that a great effort was then making in Spain and Portugal to improve the condition of the people of those countries, and that it appeared to be conducted with extraordinary moderation. It need scarcely be remarked that
the result has been so far very different from what was
then anticipated. Of events in that quarter of the globe,
with which we have so much intercourse and from which
we derive our origin, we have always been anxious and
interested spectators. The citizens of the United States
cherish sentiments the most friendly in favor of the
liberty and happiness of their fellow-men on that side
of the Atlantic. In the wars of the European powers in
matters relating to themselves we have never taken any
part, nor does it comport with our policy so to do. It
is only when our rights are invaded or seriously menaced
that we resent injuries or make preparation for our
defense. With the movements in this hemisphere we are
of necessity more immediately connected, and by causes
which must be obvious to all enlightened and impartial
observers. The political system of the allied powers is
essentially different in this respect from that of America.
This difference proceeds from that which exists in their
respective Governments; and to the defense of our own,

which has been achieved by the loss of so much blood and treasure, and matured by the wisdom of their most enlightened citizens, and under which we have enjoyed unexampled felicity, this whole nation is devoted. We owe it, therefore, to candor and to the amicable relations existing between the United States and those powers to declare that we should consider any attempt on their part to extend their system to any portion of this hemisphere as dangerous to our peace and safety. With the existing colonies or dependencies of any European power we have not interfered and shall not interfere. But with the Governments who have declared their independence and maintained it, and whose independence we have, on great consideration and just principles, acknowledged, we could not view any interposition for the purpose of oppressing them, or controlling in any other manner their destiny, by any European power in any other light than as the manifestation of an unfriendly disposition toward the United States. . . .

The late events in Spain and Portugal show that Europe is still unsettled. Of this important fact no stronger proof can be adduced than that the allied powers should have thought it proper, on any principle satisfactory to themselves, to have interposed by force in the internal concerns of Spain. To what extent such interposition may be carried, on the same principle, is a question in which all independent powers whose governments differ from theirs are interested, even those most remote, and surely none more so than the United States. Our policy in regard to Europe, which was adopted at an early stage of the wars which have so long agitated that quarter of the globe, nevertheless remains the same, which is, not to interfere in the internal concerns of any of its powers; to consider the government *de facto* as the legitimate government for us; to cultivate friendly relations with it, and to preserve those relations by a frank, firm, and manly policy, meeting in all instances the just claims of every power, submitting to injuries from none. But in regard to those continents circumstances are eminently and conspicuously different. It is impossible that the allied powers should extend their political system to any portion of either continent with-

out endangering our peace and happiness; nor can anyone believe that our southern brethren, if left to themselves, would adopt it of their own accord. It is equally
impossible, therefore, that we should behold such interposition in any form with indifference. If we look to
the comparative strength and resources of Spain and
those new Governments, and their distance from each
other, it must be obvious that she can never subdue them.
It is still the true policy of the United States to leave
the parties to themselves, in the hope that other powers
will pursue the same course. . . .

— 15 —

THE JULY ORDINANCES, JULY 25, 1830[24]

*The statesmen of Vienna restored absolutism in France
in the person of Louis XVIII, old, obese, and suffering
from gout. The Constitutional Charter of 1814, however,
granted freedom of speech, whereupon a veritable war of
words took place among monarchists, Bonapartists, republicans, ultramontanes, and anticlericals, all of whom
sought to change the government for their respective interests. Charles X (1757-1836), a man of violent and
harsh disposition who succeeded to the throne in 1824,
was determined to restore divine-right monarchy, feudal
aristocracy, and clerical domination. This fanatical Bour-
bon, who had learned nothing and forgotten nothing,
succeeded only in crystallizing nationwide sentiment
against his reactionary policies.*

[24] J. B. Duvergier, ed., *et al.*, *Collection complète des lois,
décrets, ordonnances, règlements, avis du Conseil d'État,*
2nd ed., 31 vols. (Paris, 1834-), XXX, 74-78.

On July 25, 1830, Charles X issued the July Ordinances, which suspended the freedom of the press, dissolved the newly elected Chamber of Deputies, and established an electoral system disfranchising three-fourths of the voters. The Parisian crowds reacted spontaneously. Surging to the barricades, they fought the feebly-led government troops in the narrow streets. Charles was forced to abdicate within a fortnight and fled to England. The Chamber of Deputies promptly declared the throne vacant and offered it to Louis Philippe, Duke of Orléans.

1   1   1

A

Ordinance for Suspending Liberty of the Press

Charles, etc. . . .

In conformance with the report of our Council of Ministers,

We have decreed and do decree as follows:

1. The liberty of the periodical press is hereby suspended.

2. . . . No newspaper or periodical or semiperiodical work, established or to be established, without discrimination as to their contents, shall appear, either in Paris or in the Departments, except by authorization which the authors and the printer shall have obtained separately from us.

This authorization must be renewed every three months.

It can be revoked.

3. The authorization can be granted temporarily and temporarily withdrawn by the prefects for newspapers and periodicals or semiperiodicals published or to be published in their Departments.

4. Newspapers and works published in violation of Article 2 shall be seized at once. The presses and the type which have been used for their printing shall be placed in a public repository under seal or put out of service.

5. No work containing less than twenty pages can appear without the authorization of our Minister-Secre-

tary of State of the Interior of Paris, and of the prefects of the Departments.

Any work of more than twenty printed pages which
does not constitute a connected work shall similarly be
subject to the necessity for authorization.

Works published without authorization shall be seized
at once. The presses and the type which have been used
for their printing shall be placed in a public repository
under seal or put out of service.

6. Proceedings on law suits and the transactions of
scientific or literary societies are subject to prior authorization, if they consist in whole or in part of political
matters, in which case the measures mentioned in Article
5 shall be applicable to them.

7. Any provisions contrary to the present provisions
are hereby declared to be without force. . . .

B

Ordinance for Dissolving the Chamber of Deputies

Charles, etc.

In view of Article 50 of the Constitutional Charter,
Having learned of the maneuvers that have been practiced at many places in our kingdom to deceive and
mislead the electors during the recent operations of the
electoral colleges;

Our Council having been heard;

We have decreed and do decree as follows:

1. The Chamber of Deputies is hereby dissolved.

2. Our Minister-Secretary of State of the Interior is
charged, etc. . . .

C

3. Ordinance concerning the Elections

Being determined to prevent the recurrence of the
maneuvers that have resulted in a pernicious influence
during the recent proceedings of the electoral bodies; and
wishing, therefore, in conformity with the principles of
the Constitutional Charter, to reform the rules of election, which in our experience has caused inconveniences,
we have recognized the necessity of making use of the

right which is ours to provide by our acts for the safety of the state and for the suppression of any moves to attack the dignity of our Crown. [*The subsequent thirty articles limit the franchise by ordaining higher property qualifications for voting and rigid rules for the conduct of elections.*]

— 16 —

THE ENGLISH REFORM BILLS OF 1832, 1867, AND 1884

Early nineteenth-century England was burdened by an archaic electoral and representative system even though the center of English population had shifted from the Channel ports and the south to the Midlands and the coal and iron regions of the north. There were persistent evils: "pocket boroughs" ("carried in the pocket" of a political leader), "rotten boroughs" (small villages with a voting population of five or ten still sending the traditional two burgesses to Parliament), and "borough-mongering" (buying and selling seats in Parliament).

The Reform Act of 1832, passed only after a fierce struggle, eliminated the rotten boroughs or made them smaller, gave the franchise to tenant farmers and merchants, and provided representation for the larger cities of northern England. The number of voters was increased from about 430,000 to 650,000.

The Representation of the People Act of 1867, "the second installment of democracy," gave the vote to the artisans in the boroughs, abolished eleven remaining rotten boroughs, and reduced 35 boroughs from two seats to one in the House of Commons.

The third reform bill, Representation of the People

Act of 1884, gave the vote to self-supporting, unskilled laborers and servants in both boroughs and counties. Some two million new voters were added to the rolls. Thus, England, with a "fully democratized electorate," finally became a democracy in the sense that all self-supporting men now had the right to vote. The Reform Bill of 1918 granted the vote to all women over the age of thirty; and the Reform Bill of 1928 extended the franchise to all women over twenty-one.

Following are the key provisions of the three major English Reform Acts of the nineteenth century.

✓   ✓   ✓

A

The Reform Act of 1832 [25]

An act to amend the representation of the people in England and Wales. Whereas it is expedient to take effectual measures for correcting divers abuses that have long prevailed in the choice of members to serve in the commons house of parliament; to deprive many inconsiderable places of the right of returning members; to grant such privilege to large, populous, and wealthy towns; to increase the number of knights of the shire; to extend the elective franchise to many of his majesty's subjects who have not heretofore enjoyed the same; and to diminish the expense of elections: be it therefore enacted that each of the boroughs enumerated in the schedule marked A to this act annexed [*56 boroughs*] shall, from and after the end of this present parliament, cease to return any member or members to serve in parliament.

And be it enacted that each of the boroughs enumerated in the schedule marked B [*30 boroughs*] shall return one member and no more to serve in parliament.

And be it enacted that each of the places named in the schedule marked C [*22 places*] shall for the purpose of this act be a borough, and shall return two members to serve in parliament.

[25] *Statutes of the United Kingdom,* LXII, 154 ff., 2 William IV, c. 45.

And be it enacted that each of the places named in the schedule marked D [*20 places*] shall for the purpose of this act be a borough, and shall return one member to serve in parliament. . . .

And be it enacted that every male person of full age and not subject to any legal incapacity who shall be seised at law or in equity of any lands or tenements of copyhold, or any other tenure whatever except freehold, for his own life or for the life of another or for any lives whatsoever . . . , of the clear yearly value of not less than 10 pounds . . . shall be entitled to vote in the election of a knight or knights of the shire. . . .

And be it enacted that every male person of full age and not subject to any legal incapacity who shall be entitled, either as lessee or assignee, to any lands or tenements . . . for the unexpired residue . . . of any term originally created for a period of not less than sixty years . . . of the clear yearly value of not less than ten pounds, or for the unexpired residue . . . of any term originally created for a period of not less than twenty years . . . of the clear yearly value of not less than fifty pounds, or who shall occupy as tenant any lands or tenements for which he shall be *bone fide* liable to a yearly rental of not less than fifty pounds, shall be entitled to vote in the election of a knight or knights of the shire. . . .

And be it enacted that, in every city or borough which shall return a member or members to serve in any future parliament, every male person of full age and not subject to any legal incapacity who shall occupy within such city or borough . . . , as owner or tenant any house . . . or other building . . . of the clear yearly value of not less than ten pounds shall, if duly registered . . . , be entitled to vote in the election of a member or members to serve in any future parliament for such city and borough. . . .

And be it enacted that . . . all booths erected for the convenience of taking polls shall be erected at the joint and equal expense of the several candidates. . . .

. . . Nothing in this act contained shall . . . in any wise affect the election of members to serve in parliament for the universities of Oxford or Cambridge.

B

The Reform Act of 1867: Representation of the People Act, 1867 [26]

Every man shall, in and after the year 1868, be entitled to be registered as a voter and, when registered, to vote for a member or members to serve in parliament for a borough, who is qualified as follows: that is to say, (1) is of full age, and not subject to any legal incapacity; and (2) is on the last day of July in any year and has during the preceding twelve calendar months been an inhabitant occupier, as owner or tenant, of any dwelling-house within the borough; and (3) has during the time of such occupation been rated as an ordinary occupier in respect of the premises so occupied by him within the borough to all rates, if any, made for the relief of the poor in respect of such premises; and (4) has, on or before the twentieth day of July in the same year, *bone fide* paid an equal amount in the pound to that payable by other ordinary occupiers in respect of all poor rates that have become payable by him in respect of the said premises up to the preceding fifth day of January. Provided, that no man shall under this section be entitled to be registered as a voter by reason of his being a joint occupier of any dwelling-house.

Every man shall, in and after the year 1868, be entitled to be registered as a voter and, when registered, to vote for a member or members to serve in parliament for a borough, who is qualified as follows: that is to say, (1) is of full age and not subject to any legal incapacity; and (2) as a lodger has occupied in the same borough separately and as sole tenant for the twelve months preceding the last day of July in any year the same lodgings, such lodgings being part of one and the same dwelling-house, and of a clear yearly value, if let unfurnished, of ten pounds or upwards; and (3) has resided in such lodgings during the twelve months immediately preceding the last day of July, and has claimed to be registered as a voter at the next ensuing registration of voters. . . .

[26] *Public General Statutes*, II, 1082 ff., 30-31 Victoria, c. 102.

From and after the end of the present parliament, no borough which had a less population than 10,000 at the census of 1861 shall return more than one member to serve in parliament. . . .

C

The Reform Act of 1884:
Representation of the People Act, 1884 [27]

A uniform household franchise and a uniform lodger franchise at elections shall be established in all counties and boroughs throughout the united kingdom, and every man possessed of a household qualification or a lodger qualification shall, if the qualifying premises be situate in a county in England or Scotland, be entitled to be registered as a voter and when registered to vote at an election for such county. . . .

Every man occupying any land or tenement in a county or borough in the united kingdom of a clear yearly value of not less than ten pounds shall be entitled to be registered as a voter and when registered to vote at an election for such county or borough in respect of such occupation subject to the like conditions respectively as a man is, at the passing of this act, entitled to be registered as a voter and to vote at an election for such county in respect of the county occupation franchise, and at an election for such borough in respect of the borough occupation franchise. . . .

[27] *Public General Statutes,* XXXI, 3 ff., 48 Victoria, c. 3.

17

INTERNATIONAL TREATY GUARANTEEING THE NEUTRALITY OF BELGIUM, APRIL 19, 1839[28]

At London, on April 19, 1839, a treaty was signed between Great Britain, Austria, France, Prussia, and Russia, on the one part, and The Netherlands, on the other, in which the union between Holland and Belgium, established at Vienna in 1815, was formally dissolved. A similar treaty was signed with Belgium. In the annex to the first treaty, and repeated in the second, was an article that guaranteed the independence and neutrality of Belgium. This guarantee was re-stated in a treaty between Great Britain and Prussia signed at London, on August 9, 1870.

The 1839 treaty was to have momentous consequences in 1914. After German troops crossed the Belgian border on the morning of August 4, 1914, Sir E. Goschen, the British Ambassador in Berlin, called on Chancellor von Bethmann-Hollweg for a final interview. "I found the Chancellor very agitated," Goschen reported. "His Excellency at once began a harangue, which lasted for about twenty minutes. He said that the step taken by His Majesty's Government was terrible to a degree; just for a word—'neutrality,' a word which in war time had so often been disregarded—just for a scrap of paper Great Britain was going to make war on a kindred nation who desired nothing better than to be friends with her." The "scrap of paper," signed by Palmerston, Senff, Sebastiani, Bülow, and di Borgo in 1839, is reproduced here.

[28] E. Hertslet, ed., *The Map of Europe by Treaty* (London, 1875), II, 982-85.

Annex to the Treaty signed at London, on the 19th of April, 1839, between Great Britain, Austria, France, Prussia, and Russia, on the one part, and the Netherlands, on the other part

ARTICLE 1. The Belgian Territory shall be composed of the Provinces of: South Brabant; Liege; Namur; Hainault; West Flanders; East Flanders; Antwerp; and Leimburg; such as they formed part of the United Kingdom of the Netherlands in 1815, with the exception of those districts of the Province of Limburg which are designated in Article 4.

The Belgian Territory shall, moreover, comprise that part of the Grand Duchy of Luxemburg which is specified in Article 2.

ARTICLE 2. In the Grand Duchy of Luxemburg, the limits of the Belgian Territory shall be such as will hereinafter be described. . . .

ARTICLE 4. In execution of that part of Article 1 which relates to the Province of Limburg, and in consequence of the cessions which His Majesty the King of the Netherlands, Grand Duke of Luxemburg, makes in Article 2, His said Majesty shall possess, either to be held by him in his character of Grand Duke of Luxemburg, or for the purpose of being united to Holland, those Territories, the limits of which are hereinafter described. . . .

ARTICLE 7. Belgium, within the limits specified in Articles 1, 2, and 4, shall form an Independent and perpetually Neutral State. It shall be bound to observe such Neutrality towards all other States. . . .

18

REPORT OF LORD ASHLEY'S MINES COMMISSION, 1842 [29]

The conditions existing in the British mines during the early eighteen forties were shocking and scandalous. Mingled among naked men chopping at the veins of the earth were young girls crawling on all fours and tugging small coal carts. Others sat in darkness and "trapped," opening and closing doors for the passage of the carts. Working underground for long hours, and for pitifully low wages, these children seldom saw the light of day. The atrocities visited upon them resulted in lung diseases, ruined eyesight, and nervous collapse. Laissez faire *had truly become "the dismal science."*

The conscience of England was lashed by the novelist, Charles Dickens, and the fiery pamphleteer, William Cobbett, whose social tracts denounced the exploitation of workers in mines and factories. With public attention drawn to the degrading situation, Parliament was prevailed upon to interfere. Three Tory members, Michael Sadler, Richard Oastler, and Lord Ashley, led parliamentary investigations of the iniquitous conditions in factories and mines, leading to a number of reforms for the industrial workers.

The following excerpts give the testimony of four English girls during the investigation of labor conditions in mines made by Lord Ashley's Mines Commission in 1842. As a result of this inquiry, the Mines Act of 1842 excluded boys under eleven, together with all girls and women, from further employment in the coal pits. By 1846 no child under nine was permitted to work in mines. But there was still no limit on the hours for boys or men in the mines.

[29] *Parliamentary Papers, 1842,* XV-XVIII, appendix I, pp. 252, 258, 439, 461; appendix II, pp. 107, 122, 205.

A

Sarah Gooder, aged 8 years

I'm a trapper in the Gawber pit. It does not tire me, but I have to trap without a light, and I'm scared. I go at four and sometimes half past three in the morning, and come out at five and half past. I never go to sleep. Sometimes I sing when I've light, but not in the dark; I dare not sing then. I don't like being in the pit. I am very sleepy when I go sometimes in the morning. I go to Sunday-school and read "Reading made Easy." [*She knows her letters and can read little words.*] They teach me to pray. [*She repeated the Lord's prayer, not very perfectly, and ran on with the following addition: "God bless my father and mother, and sister and brother, uncles and aunts and cousins, and everybody else, and God bless me and make me a good servant. Amen."*] I have heard tell of Jesus many a time. I don't know why he came on earth, I'm sure, and I don't know why he died, but he had stones for his head to rest on. I would like to be at school far better than in the pit.

B

Isabella Read, 12 years old, coal-bearer

I am brought with sister and brother, it is very sore work; cannot say how many rakes or journeys I make from pit's bottom to wall face and back.

I carry out about 1 cwt. and a quarter on my back; have to stoop so much and creep through water, which is frequently up to the calves of my legs.

I do not like the work, nor do the lassies, but they are made to like it.

C

Mary Barrett, aged 14

I have worked down in pit five years. Father is working next pit. I have 12 brothers and sisters—all of them but one live at home. They weave, and wind, and hurry, and one is a counter, one of them can read, none of the rest can, or write. They never went to day-school, but three of them go to Sunday-school. I hurry for my brother John, and come down at seven o'clock about. I go up at six, sometimes even seven. I do not like working in pit, but I am obliged to get a living. I work always without stockings, or shoes, or trousers. I wear nothing but my chemise. I have to go up to the headings with the men. They are all naked there; I am got well used to that, and don't care much about it. I was afraid at first, and did not like it. They never behave rudely to me. I cannot read or write.

Patience Kershaw, aged 17

My father has been dead about a year. My mother is living and has ten children, five lads and five lassies; the oldest is about thirty, the youngest is four. Three lassies go to mill. All the lads are colliers, two getters and three hurriers. One lives at home and does nothing. Mother does nought but look after home.

All my sisters have been hurriers, but three went to the mill. Alice went because her legs swelled from hurrying in cold water when she was hot. I never went to day-school. I go to Sunday-school, but I cannot read or write. I go to pit at five o'clock in the morning and come out at five in the evening. I get my breakfast of porridge and milk first. I take my dinner with me, a cake, and eat it as I go. I do not stop or rest any time for the purpose. I get nothing else until I get home, and then have potatoes and meat, not every day meat. I hurry in the clothes I have now got on, trousers and ragged jacket.

The bald place upon my head is made by thrusting the corves.[30] My legs have never swelled, but sisters' did when they went to the mill. I hurry the corves a mile and more underground and back; they weigh 300 cwt.; I hurry 11 a-day. I wear a belt and chain at the workings to get the corves out. The getters that I work for are

---

[30] Plural of corf, a low-wheeled vehicle for carrying coal in the mines.

naked except for their caps. They pull off all their clothes. I see them at work when I go up. Sometimes they beat me, if I am not quick enough, with their hands. They strike me upon the back. The boys take liberties with me; sometimes they pull me about. I am the only girl in the pit. There are about 20 boys and 15 men. All the men are naked. I would rather work in mill than in coal-pit.

[*This girl is an ignorant, filthy, ragged, and deplorable-looking object, and such a one as the uncivilized natives of the prairies would be shocked to look upon.*]

— 19 —

ANESTHESIA: THE CONQUEST OF PAIN, OCTOBER 16, 1846

On the morning of October 16, 1846 some Harvard medical students were gathered under the Bulfinch dome of the Massachusetts General Hospital, together with several of the top names in surgery, to watch Dr. John Collins Warren remove a vascular tumor from the left side of the neck of a painter named Gilbert Abbott. For the first time in history ether was administered in a surgical operation in public. The anesthetist was Dr. William Thomas Green Morton, a Boston dentist. The patient experienced no pain, merely the sensation of scraping with a blunt instrument.

Morton chose the name "Letheon," but Oliver Wendell Holmes proposed the word "Anesthesia," which was accepted by the medical world. Morton's later life was embittered by a torrent of controversy and litigation

*which reduced him to financial straits. Today he is rec-
ognized as one of the world's great benefactors—the
man who conquered pain.*

*The agony of a surgical operation before anesthesia
was described in a letter written to Sir James Simpson
by a doctor who had to have a limb amputated. (See the
first selection below.) The first public operation was
described by an eyewitness, Dr. Washington Ayer of
San Francisco. (See the second selection.)*

✓   ✓   ✓

A

An Operation before Anesthesia [31]

I at once agreed to submit to the operation, but asked
a week to prepare for it, not with the slightest expectation that the disease would take a favorable turn in the
interval, or that the anticipated horrors of the operation
would become less appalling by reflection upon them, but
simply because it was so probable that the operation
would be followed by a fatal issue that I wished to prepare for death, and what lies beyond it, whilst my faculties were clear and my emotions were completely undisturbed.

The week, so slow and yet so swift in its passage, at
length came to an end, and the morning of the operation
arrived. The operation was a more tedious one than
some which involve much greater mutilation. It necessitated cruel cutting through inflamed and morbidly sensi-
tive parts, and could not be despatched by a few strokes
of the knife.

Of the agony it occasioned I will say nothing. Suffering so great as I underwent cannot be expressed in
words, and thus fortunately cannot be recalled. The
particular pangs are now forgotten; but the blank whirl-
wind of emotion, the horror of great darkness, and the
sense of desertion by God and man, bordering close upon
despair, which swept through my mind and overwhelmed
my heart, I can never forget, however gladly I would
do so. Only the wish to save others some of my suffer-

[31] From Sir James Simpson's *Memoirs* (n.d.)

ings makes me deliberately recall and confess the anguish and humiliation of such a personal experience, nor can I find language more sober or familiar than that which I have used to express feelings which, happily for us all, are too rare as matters of general experience to have been shaped in the household words.

During the operation, in spite of the pain it occasioned, my senses were preternaturally acute, as I have been told they generally are in patients under such circumstances. I watched all that the surgeon did with a fascinated intensity.

I still recall with unwelcome vividness the spreading out of the instruments, the twisting of the tourniquet, the first incision, the fingering of the sawed bone, the sponge pressed on the flap, the tying of the blood vessels, the stitching of the skin, and the bloody dismembered limb lying on the floor. Those are not pleasant remembrances. For a long time they haunted me, and even now they are easily resusicated; and though they cannot bring back the suffering attending the events which gave them a place in my memory, they can occasion a suffering of their own, and be the cause of a disquiet which favors neither mental nor bodily health.

B

*The First Public Operation under
Anesthesia, October 16, 1846* [32]

The day arrived; the time appointed was noted on the dial, when the patient was led into the operating-room, and Dr. Warren, with a board of the most eminent surgeons in the State were gathered around the sufferer. All is ready—the stillness oppressive. It had been announced that a test of some preparation was to be made, for which the *astonishing* claim had been made, that it would render the person operated upon free from pain. Those present were incredulous, and as Dr. Morton had not arrived at the time appointed, and fifteen minutes had passed, Dr. Warren said, with significant meaning:

"I presume he is otherwise engaged."

[32] *Occidental Medical Times,* March, 1896.

This was followed with a derisive laugh, and Dr. Warren grasped his knife and was about to proceed with the operation; at that moment Dr. Morton entered a side door, when Dr. Warren turned to him, and in a strong voice said:

"Well, Sir, your patient is ready."

In a few minutes he was ready for the surgeon's knife, when Dr. Morton said:

"*Your* patient is ready, Sir."

The operation was for a congenital tumor on the left side of the neck, extending along the jaw to the maxillary gland and into the mouth, embracing the margin of the tongue. The operation was successful; and when the patient recovered he declared that he had suffered no pain.

Dr. Warren then turned to those present and said:

"*Gentlemen, this is no humbug.*"

The conquest of pain had been achieved.

— 20 —

PROCLAMATIONS OF THE FRENCH PROVISIONAL GOVERNMENT, FEBRUARY-MARCH, 1848

From 1830 to 1848 France was a constitutional monarchy, ruled by the "bourgeois king," Louis Philippe. A widespread depression in the years 1846-47 increased unrest and revolutionary agitation. In the early months of 1848 Louis Philippe's position became untenable. When the government prohibited a great public banquet that had been planned by the opposition parties for February 22, 1848, angry crowds in Paris went to the barricades and called for the dismissal of the reactionary Guizot ministry. The Government called out the National Guard, but the latter joined the insurgents in their march on the Tuileries. On February 24, 1848, like Charles X before him, Louis Philippe abdicated. Disguised as "Mr. Smith," he fled to England, the traditional home of discredited French royalty.

The Provisional Government, under pressure by the Parisian crowds, issued one proclamation and decree after another defining the new government, providing for electoral reform, and inaugurating radical social measures. This prodigious activity in proclamations is indicated in the following documents. Note the attempts to meet the demands of the socialists and to implement the principles of Liberty, Equality, and Fraternity. Despite their promises, however, the majority of the members of the Provisional Government opposed labor reforms. The national workshops soon collapsed, due to incompetent direction and governmental indifference. When the National Assembly set up General Cavaignac as a "republican dictator," backed by the National Guard, the bloodiest street fighting Europe had ever seen broke out towards the end of June, 1848.

✓   ✓   ✓

A

First Proclamation of the Provisional Government, February 24, 1848 [33]

IN THE NAME OF THE FRENCH PEOPLE!

A retrograde Government has been overturned by the heroism of the people of Paris. This Government has fled, leaving behind it trails of blood, which will forever forbid its return.

The blood of the people has flowed, as in July, but, happily, it has not been shed in vain. It has secured a national and popular government, in accordance with the rights, the progress, and the will of this great and generous people.

A Provisional Government, at the call of the people and some Deputies in the sitting of the 24th of February, is for the moment invested with the care of organizing

[33] *Annual Register, 1848* (London, 1849), pp. 239-40.

and securing the national victory. It is composed of MM. Dupont (d l'Eure), Lamartine, Crémieux, Arago, Ledru Rollin, and Garnier Pagès. The Secretaries to this Government are MM. Armand Marrast, Louis Blanc, and Ferdinand Flocon. These citizens have not hesitated for an instant to accept the patriotic mission which had been imposed upon them by the urgency of the occasion.

Frenchmen, give the world the example Paris has given to France! Prepare yourselves, by order and confidence in yourselves, for the constitutions which are about to be given to you.

The Provisional Government desires a Republic, pending the ratification of the French people, who are to be immediately consulted. Neither the people of France nor the Provisional Government desire to substitute their opinion for the opinions of the citizens at large, upon the definite form of government which the national sovereignty shall proclaim.

L'unité de la nation, formed henceforth of all classes of the people who compose it;

The government of the nation by itself;

Liberty, Equality, Fraternity for its principles;

The people to devise and maintain order.

Such is the Democratic Government which France owes to herself, and which our efforts will assure to her.

Such are the first acts of the Provisional Government.

(Signed)
DUPONT (DE L'EURE)
LAMARTINE
LEDRU ROLLIN
BÉDEAU
MICHEL GOUDCHAUX
ARAGO
BETHMONT MARIE
CARNOT
CAVAIGNAC
GARNIER PAGÈS

The Municipal Guard is disbanded.

The protection of the city of Paris is confided to the National Guard, under the orders of M. Courtais.

B

Declaration Relative to Workingmen,
February 25, 1848 [34]

IN THE NAME OF THE FRENCH PEOPLE!

The Government of the French Republic engages to guarantee the subsistence of the workman by his labor.

It engages to guarantee work to all citizens.

It recognizes the right of workmen to combine for the purpose of enjoying the lawful proceeds of their labor.

The Provisional Government restores to the workmen, *to whom it belongs,* the million of the Civil List now due.

C

Proclamation of the Republic,
February 26, 1848 [35]

Citizens!

Royalty, under whatsoever form it may take, is abolished.

No more legitimism, no more Bonapartism, no regency.

The Provisional Government has taken all the necessary measures to make it impossible for the former dynasty to return or to introduce a new dynasty.

The Republic is proclaimed.

The people are united.

All the forts which surround the capital are ours.

The courageous garrison of Vincennes is a garrison of brothers.

Let us preserve that old republican flag whose three colors made with our fathers the tour of the world.

Let us show that this symbol of Liberty, Equality, and Fraternity is at the same time the symbol of order, and of order the more real and lasting, since justice is its foundation and the entire people its instrument.

[34] *Annual Register, 1848* (London, 1849), p. 240.
[35] Duvergier, J. B., *et al., Collection complète des lois, décrets, ordonnances, règlements, avis du Conseil d'État,* 2nd ed., 31 vols. (Paris, 1834-   ), XLVIII, 60.

The people have already understood that the provisioning of Paris, and the hands which erected the barricades, have in several places made in the barricades an opening large enough for the free passage of wagons.

Let this example be followed everywhere. Let Paris resume its accustomed appearance and commerce, its activity, and its confidence. Let the people at the same time look to the maintenance of their rights. And let them continue to assure, as they have done until now, the public peace and security.

D

Decree for the Establishment of Workshops, February 26, 1848 [36]

IN THE NAME OF THE FRENCH PEOPLE!
The Provisional Government of the Republic
Decrees the immediate establishment of national workshops.

The Minister of Public Works is charged with the execution of this decree.

E

Decree Abolishing Titles of Nobility, February 29, 1848 [37]

IN THE NAME OF THE FRENCH PEOPLE!
The Provisional Government,
Considering that equality is one of the three great principles of the French Republic, that, in consequence, it ought to receive an immediate realization,

Decrees:—

All the former titles of nobility are abolished; the designations which were connected with them are prohibited; they cannot be taken in public nor be mentioned in any public document.

[36] Duvergier, *op. cit.*, XLVIII, 60.
[37] Duvergier, *op. cit.*, XLVIII, 64.

F

Decree on Labor, March 2, 1848 [38]

IN THE NAME OF THE FRENCH PEOPLE!

Upon the report of the Provisional Government for the workers:

Considering:

1. That too prolonged manual labor ruins the health of the worker, but, in addition, prevents him from cultivating his intelligence, and thereby impairs the dignity of man;

2. That the exploitation of the workers by the working sub-contractors—the *marchandeurs,* or *tâcherons*—is essentially unjust, vexatious, and opposed to the principle of fraternity;

The Provisional Government of the Republic decrees:

1. The working day is shortened by one hour. Therefore, in Paris, where it was eleven hours, it is reduced to ten; and in the provinces, where it has been until now twelve hours, it is reduced to eleven;

2. The exploitations of the workers by the sub-contractors, or *marchandage,* is hereby abolished.

It is understood that the associations of the workers which have not for their purpose the exploitation of workers by each other are not considered as *marchandage.*

G

Decree for the National Assembly,
March 5, 1848 [39]

1. The National Assembly shall decree the Constitution.

2. The election shall have the population for its basis.

3. The representatives of the people shall come to 900.

4. The suffrage shall be direct and universal, without any limitations as to property.

5. All Frenchmen of the age of 21 years shall be electors. . . .

6. The ballot shall be secret. . . .

[38] Duvergier, *op cit.,* XLVIII, 67.
[39] *Annual Register, 1848* (London, 1849), pp. 245-46.

THE COMMUNIST MANIFESTO, 1848 [40]

The essentials of Marxian theory were set forth in the Communist Manifesto issued in 1848 by an organization known as the Communist League. It was drawn up by Karl Marx (1818-1883) and Friedrich Engels (1820-1895) as a kind of party platform for an international gathering of workingmen in London. The pamphlet traced the history of the working-class movement, surveyed critically the existing socialist literature, and explained the outlines of communism. Starting with the materialistic interpretation of history and using Mill's labor theory of value, Marx and Engels spoke of an inescapable class struggle, the inevitable triumph of the proletariat, and the establishment of the Communist state. Further elaboration of the main elements of Marxian theory was made in Marx's monumental work, Das Kapital *(1867-1894). Following are extracts from the Communist Manifesto.*

✓ ✓ ✓

A SPECTRE is haunting Europe—the spectre of Communism. All the powers of old Europe have entered into a holy alliance to exorcise this spectre; Pope and Czar, Metternich and Guizot, French Radicals and German police-spies.

Where is the party in opposition that has not been decried as communistic by its opponents in power? Where the Opposition that has not hurled back the branding reproach of Communism, against the more advanced oppo-

[40] Karl Marx and Friedrich Engels, *Manifesto of the Communist Party,* authorized English translation, edited and annotated by Friedrich Engels (Charles S. Kerr and Company, Chicago, n.d.), pp. 1-59, *passim.*

sition parties, as well as against its reactionary adversaries?

Two things result from this fact.

I. Communism is already acknowledged by all European Powers to be itself a Power.

II. It is high time that Communists should openly, in the face of the whole world, publish their views, their aims, their tendencies, and meet this nursery tale of the Spectre of Communism with a Manifesto of the party itself.

To this end, Communists of various nationalities have assembled in London, and sketched the following manifesto, to be published in the English, French, German, Italian, Flemish and Danish languages. . . .

1. Bourgeois and Proletarians

The history of all hitherto existing society is the history of class struggles.

Freeman and slave, patrician and plebeian, lord and serf, guild-master and journeyman, in a word, oppressor and oppressed, stood in constant opposition to one another, carried on an uninterrupted, now hidden, now open fight, a fight that each time ended, either in a revolutionary reconstitution of society at large, or in the common ruin of the contending classes. . . .

The modern bourgeois society that has sprouted from the ruins of feudal society, has not done away with class antagonisms. It has but established new classes, new conditions of oppression, new forms of struggle in place of the old ones.

Our epoch, the epoch of the bourgeoisie, possesses this distinctive feature; it has simplified the class antagonisms. Society as a whole is more and more splitting up into two great classes directly facing each other: Bourgeoisie and Proletariat. . . .

The bourgeoisie, wherever it has got the upper hand, has put an end to all feudal, patriarchal, idyllic relations. It has pitilessly torn asunder the motley feudal ties that bound man to his "natural superiors," and has left remaining no other nexus between man and man than naked self-interest, than callous "cash payment." It has drowned the most heavenly ecstasies of religious fervor, of chivalrous enthusiasm, of philistine sentimentalism, in the icy water of egotistical calculation. It has resolved personal worth into exchange value, and in place of the numberless indefeasible chartered freedoms, has set up that single, unconscionable freedom—Free Trade. In one word, for exploitation, veiled by religious and political illusions, it has substituted naked, shameless, direct, brutal exploitation. . .

But not only has the bourgeoisie forged the weapons that bring death to itself; it has also called into existence the men who are to wield those weapons—the modern working class—the proletarians.

In proportion as the bourgeoisie, i.e., capital, is developed, in the same proportion is the proletariat, the modern working-class, developed, a class of laborers, who live only so long as they find work, and who find work only so long as their labor increases capital. These laborers, who must sell themselves piecemeal, are a commodity, like every other article of commerce, and are consequently exposed to all the vicissitudes of competition, to all the fluctuations of the market. . . .

But with the development of industry the proletariat not only increases in number, it becomes concentrated in greater masses, its strength grows, and it feels that strength more. The various interests and conditions of life within the ranks of the proletariat are more and more equalized, in proportion as machinery obliterates all distinctions of labor, and nearly everywhere reduces wages to the same low level. The growing competition among the bourgeois, and the resulting commercial crisis, make the wages of the workers ever more fluctuating. The unceasing improvement of machinery, ever more rapidly developing, makes their livelihood more and more precarious; the collisions between individual workmen and individual bourgeois take more and more the character of collisions between two classes. Thereupon the workers begin to form combinations (Trades' Unions) against the bourgeois; they club together in order to keep up wages; they found permanent associations in order to make provision beforehand for these occasional revolts. Here and there the contest breaks into riots. . . .

2. Proletarians and Communists

In what relation do the Communists stand to the proletarians as a whole?

The Communists do not form a separate party opposed to other working-class parties.

They have no interests separate and apart from those of the proletariat as a whole.

They do not set up any sectarian principles of their own, by which to shape and mould the proletarian movement.

The Communists are distinguished from the other working class parties by this only: 1. In the national struggles of the proletarians of the different countries, they point out and bring to the front the common interests of the entire proletariat independently of all nationality. 2. In the various stages of development which the struggle of the working class against the bourgeoisie has to pass through, they always and everywhere represent the interests of the movement as a whole. . . .

The immediate aim of the Communists is the same as that of all the other proletarian parties: formation of the proletariat into a class, overthrow of the bourgeois supremacy, conquest of political power by the proletariat. . . .

The distinguishing feature of Communism is not the abolition of property generally, but the abolition of bourgeois property. But modern bourgeois private property is the final and most complete expression of the system of producing and appropriating products, that is based on class antagonism, on the exploitation of the many by the few.

In this sense, the theory of the Communists may be summed up in the single sentence: Abolition of private property. . . .

The proletariat will use its political supremacy, to wrest, by degrees, all capital from the bourgeoisie, to centralize all instruments of production in the hands of the State, i.e., of the proletariat organized as the ruling class; and to increase the total of productive forces as rapidly as possible.

Of course, in the beginning, this cannot be effected except by means of despotic inroads on the rights of property, and on the conditions of bourgeois production; by means of measures, therefore, which appear economically insufficient and untenable, but which, in the course of the movement, outstrip themselves, necessitate further inroads upon the old social order, and are unavoidable as a means of entirely revolutionizing the mode of production.

These measures will of course be different in different countries.

Nevertheless in the most advanced countries the following will be pretty generally applicable:

1. Abolition of property in land and application of all rents of land to public purposes.

2. A heavy progressive or graduated income tax.

3. Abolition of all right of inheritance.

4. Confiscation of the property of all emigrants and rebels.

5. Centralization of credit in the hands of the State, by means of a national bank with State capital and exclusive monopoly.

6. Centralization of the means of communication and transport in the hands of the State.

7. Extension of factories and instruments of production owned by the State; the bringing into cultivation of waste lands, and the improvement of the soil generally in accordance with a common plan.

8. Equal liability of all to labor. Establishment of industrial armies, especially for agriculture.

9. Combination of agriculture with manufacturing industries; gradual abolition of the distinction between town and country, by a more equable distribution of population over the country.

10. Free education for all children in public schools. Abolition of children's factory labor in its present form. Combination of education with industrial production, etc., etc. . . .

In place of the old bourgeois society, with its classes and class antagonisms, we shall have an association, in which the free development of each is the condition for the free development of all. . . .

4. Position of the Communist in Relation to the Various Existing Opposition Parties

The Communists everywhere support every revolutionary movement against the existing social and political order of things.

In all these movements they bring to the front, as the leading question in each, the property question, no matter what its degree of development at the time.

Finally, they labor everywhere for the union and agreement of the democratic parties of all countries.

The Communists disdain to conceal their views and aims. They openly declare that their ends can be attained only by the forcible overthrow of all existing social conditions. Let the ruling classes tremble at a Communistic revolution. The proletarians have nothing to lose but their chains. They have a world to win.

Workingmen of all countries, unite!

— 22 —

THE OPENING OF JAPAN, MARCH 31, 1854

Portuguese navigators and Jesuit missionaries tried to establish a foothold in Japan in the sixteenth century, but once their influence became apparent they were expelled. For centuries the Japanese remained isolated from the West. In 1850, the island-empire was a feudal state, controlled by a mikado *considered to be too sacred to mingle in ordinary affairs, and a class of fighting nobility called* samurai.

In the summer of 1853, Commodore Matthew Calbraith Perry anchored his "black ships of the evil mien" in the

Bay of Tokyo, and released the Japanese from centuries of self-imposed seclusion. A young naval officer from Philadelphia, Edward Yorke McCauley, was an eyewitness to the epoch-making mission. In his Diary *he left an account of the visits to Naha on Okinawa in August, 1853, and of the events surrounding the treaty-signing in the waters of Japan the following March. His account was subsequently documented by Townsend Harris, first American minister to Japan, who successfully negotiated a trade treaty with that country. Document B gives the full text of the treaty with Japan, March 31, 1854.*

Following the opening of Japan, the Westernization of the country proceeded rapidly. Virtually overnight, the whole structure of Japanese life was transformed from top to bottom. Reforms were inaugurated that changed Japan into a modern constitutional state, an industrial nation, and a world power.

✓   ✓   ✓

A

Eyewitness Account by Edward Yorke McCauley [41]

August 20th [1853]. We walked through the town of Naha. The streets are all paved with granite, cut in all manners of shapes, with the edges neatly fitting each other. The houses are low, and the tiles cemented together presenting a very tidy appearance. Every house is walled around seven or eight feet high, and none have a direct entrance, but by a zigzag path round little walls and fences, which, though *very good for the purpose of keeping off the spy, upon which system the government is founded,* suggests difficulties in getting an easy access home after partaking of the compliments of the season on a New Year's day, and in no way reconcilable with the object of latch keys. . . .

As we walked along, we became painfully aware of the fact of our being under the surveillance of the police. *There was a spy ahead and another astern, and as fast as we went they kept on in their stations.* If any laborers

[41] From the *McCauley Diary.* Courtesy of The New York Historical Society.

happened to be coming along the road they passed the word to them and down they would squat with their backs towards us until we passed. Shops shut up, women disappeared, as though they were a "marriage blight," and children nearly went into fits in their terror and haste to get out of sight. If we dodged the van and rear spies and made a dip into a bye lane, a mandarin had apparently done so a moment before us, quite accidentally, of course, and everybody was seen helter skelter at the bottom of the street for a moment, and then vanish, leaving everything private and marketable where it stood. . . .

The system of spying here is carried out not only on strangers arriving here, who are requested to clear out as soon as possible, but also among themselves, *every man being a spy on his neighbor, so that everything that passes is known to the mandarins,* who generally, I believe, are sent here from Japan, and are exceedingly jealous of everything they have. So that the moment one of *us* put his foot ashore, shops are closed and everything likely to interest us is put out of sight. With the islanders in general, we are great favorites. They come on board, will take anything to eat confidently, whereas on shore they will not touch it. It is true that they are all the time so scared with the guns, drums, and calls as to be enjoying a somewhat precarious existence, but when they go they grin with satisfaction and always manage to come a second time in spite of the mandarins, who never if they can help it allow the same crew to come twice lest they should be conciliated and always have them accompanied by one of their own order.

Feb. 17th [*1854*]. [*The*] Commodore, having given the natives three days to decide on giving him a reception here or at Jeddo, they came on board today in a glorious humor, saying that they had good news from Jeddo; that the treaty was to be signed and everything settled amicably. I even got a pair of the officials to come down into the steerage, where we gave them a little feed, and a glass of something to astonish their insides. But, bless my wig, they swallowed poteen, brandy, gin and saki alternately, a mixture that would swamp the d---l himself; and finally went off as happy as two such polite beings could ever get. (It wasn't the first time that party got drunk by a long shot!) Before leaving, they showed us their swords, which are certainly beautiful. The grasp is long enough to be held by both hands and something to spare.

One thing must be said of these people, which cannot be gainsaid, that they are without exception the most polite people on the face of the earth, not only on board here, but also in their boats alongside. Their intercourse with one another seemed to be of the most amiable and self-denying kind. This affects even their gestures. They are very graceful in everything except walking, which their garments deforms into a waddle. *They are very inquisitive about everything on board. They have measured the ship, guns, and every odd and end they can spy.*

March 27th [1854]. Fitted out the quarterdeck with flags, and all sorts of contrivances usual on such occasions, as bayonet, chandeliers, musket rack, candlesticks, etc., etc.

A table was set below for the Commodore and the high Commissioners, and another on deck for the lesser gents and the officers of the Squadron. This arrangement was consequent to the fact that the smaller fry are not allowed to sit, or eat in the presence of their Princes. At three their barge went alongside of the *Macedonian,* where they were shown around and saluted with seventeen guns on leaving. They then came on board here. Steam was up on one boiler. Every one of them had his paper and pencil in hand, and copied everything they could get at. One of the field pieces was worked with blank cartridges, quite surprising them by the rapidity with which they are fired. Afterwards they adjourned to dinner. Of course it was my luck to have the deck and I lost all the best part of the fun, being relieved about dessert time.

[March] 31st [1854]. Today the treaty was signed in great style, but being laid up [*with scurvy*] I am unable to go and see the instrument before it is boxed up. It appears that the port of Simoda in the principality of Idzu, Hakodaté in the principality of Matsumai, and the Napa-Kiang in the Loochoo group are to be thrown open to us at once, or rather within fifty days, and that in the course of five years, when they have gained, as they say, a little more experience in the way of foreign trade, they will throw more ports open.

B

Treaty with Japan, March 31, 1854 [42]

The United States of America and the Empire of Japan, desiring to establish firm, lasting, and sincere friendship between the two nations, have resolved to fix, in a manner clear and positive, by means of a treaty or general convention of peace and amity, the rules which shall in future be mutually observed in the intercourse of their respective countries; for which most desirable object the President of the United States has conferred full powers on his commissioner, Matthew Calbraith Perry, special ambassador of the United States to Japan, and the August Sovereign of Japan has given similar full powers to his commissioners, Hayashi, Dai-gaku-no-kami, Ido, prince of Tsus-Sima, Izawa, prince of Mimasaki, and Udono, member of the board of revenue. And the said commissioners, after having exchanged their said full powers, and duly considered the premises, have agreed to the following articles :—

ARTICLE 1. There shall be a perfect, permanent, and universal peace and a sincere and cordial amity between the United States of America on the one part, and the empire of Japan on the other part, and between their people respectively, without exception of persons of places.

ARTICLE 2. The port of Simoda, in the principality of Idzu, and the port of Hakodade, in the principality of Matsmai, are granted by the Japanese as ports for the reception of American ships, where they can be supplied with wood, water, provisions, and coal, and other articles their necessities may require, as far as the Japanese have them. The time for opening the first-named port is immediately on signing this treaty; the last-named port is to be opened immediately after the same day in the ensuing Japanese year. [*Note.*—A tariff of prices shall be given by the Japanese officers of the things they can furnish, payment for which shall be made in gold and silver coin.]

ARTICLE 3. Whenever ships of the United States are

⁴² *Statutes at Large and Treaties of the United States of America* (Boston, 1859), XI, 597-98.

thrown or wrecked on the coast of Japan, the Japanese vessels will assist them, and carry their crews to Simoda, or Hakodade, and hand them over to their countrymen appointed to receive them; whatever articles the shipwrecked men may have preserved shall likewise be restored, and the expenses incurred in the rescue and support of Americans and Japanese who may thus be thrown upon the shores of either nation are not to be refunded.

ARTICLE 4. Those shipwrecked persons and other citizens of the United States, temporarily living at Simoda and Hakodade, shall not be subject to such restrictions and confinement as the Dutch and Chinese are at Nagasaki, but shall be free at Simoda to go where they please within the limits of seven Japanese miles (or *ri*) from a small island in the harbor of Simoda, marked on the accompanying chart hereto appended; and shall in like manner be free to go where they please at Hakodade, within limits to be defined after the visit of the United States squadron to that place.

ARTICLE 6. If there be any other sort of goods wanted, or any business which shall require to be arranged, there shall be careful deliberation between the parties in order to settle such matters.

ARTICLE 7. It is agreed that ships of the United States, resorting to the ports open to them shall be permitted to exchange gold and silver coin and articles of goods for other articles of goods, under such regulations as shall be temporarily established by the Japanese government for that purpose. It is stipulated, however, that the ships of the United States shall be permitted to carry away whatever articles they are unwilling to exchange.

ARTICLE 8. Wood, water, provisions, coal, and goods required, shall only be procured through the agency of Japanese officers appointed for that purpose and in no other manner.

ARTICLE 9. It is agreed that if at any future day the government of Japan shall grant to any other nation or nations privileges and advantages which are not herein granted to the United States and the citizens thereof, that these same privileges and advantages shall be granted likewise to the United States and to the citizens thereof, without any consultation or delay.

ARTICLE 10. Ships of the United States shall be permitted to resort to no other ports in Japan but Simoda and Hakodade, unless in distress or forced by stress of weather.

ARTICLE 11. There shall be appointed, by the government of the United States, consuls or agents to reside in Simoda, at any time after the expiration of eighteen months from the date of the signing of this treaty: provided that either of the two governments deem such arrangements necessary.

ARTICLE 12. The present convention having been concluded and duly signed, shall be obligatory and faithfully observed by the United States of America and Japan, and by the citizens and subjects of each respective power; and it is to be ratified and approved by the President of the United States, by and with the advice and consent of the Senate thereof, and by the August Sovereign of Japan, and the ratification shall be exchanged within eighteen months from the date of the signature thereof, or sooner if practicable.

Done at Kanagawa this thirty-first day of March, in the year of our Lord Jesus Christ one thousand eight hundred and fifty-four, and of Kayei, the seventh year, third month, and third day.

M. C. PERRY

— 23 —

THE TREATY OF PARIS, MARCH 30, 1856[43]

The possibility of Russian expansion through the Straits to the Mediterranean led Great Britain to intervene in the Near East to checkmate Russia. Nicholas I, who had

[43] E. Hertslet, *The Map of Europe by Treaty* (London, 1875), II, pp. 1250 ff. (*passim*).

*constructed a huge fortress and naval port at Sebastopol
on the Crimean peninsula, believed that Russia was ready
to push to the Mediterranean. The immediate cause of the
Crimean War (1853-56) was a quarrel over the custody
of holy shrines in Palestine. Napoleon III appealed to the
sultan of Turkey to restore the shrines to Roman Catholic monks; Nicholas, head of the Greek Orthodox Church,
demanded that the Greek monks be left undisturbed. When
the sultan refused Russian demands as an unwarranted
interference in Turkish internal affairs, Nicholas dis-
patched Russian troops to the Turkish principalities of
Moldavia and Wallachia. Turkey declared war on October 4, 1853, and was joined by France and England on
March 28, 1854, and by Sardinia early in 1855.*

*Though the Russian army and navy fought stubbornly,
the war ended with the capitulation of Russia. The Treaty
of Paris opened the Black Sea to the commerce of the
world, declared the Danube River open to navigation by
all nations, and required Russia to respect the integrity
of the Ottoman Empire. The dictated peace, however, did
not last long.*

✦   ✦   ✦

ARTICLE 1. From the day of the exchange of the
Ratifications of the present Treaty there shall be Peace
and Friendship between Her Majesty the Queen of the
United Kingdom of Great Britain and Ireland, His Majesty the Emperor of the French, His Majesty the King
of Sardinia, His Imperial Majesty the Sultan, on the one
part, and His Majesty the Emperor of all the Russians,
on the other part; as well as between their heirs and successors, their respective dominions and subjects, in perpetuity.

ARTICLE 2. Peace being happily re-established between their said Majesties, the Territories conquered or
occupied by their armies during the War will be reciprocally evacuated.

Special arrangements shall regulate the mode of the
Evacuation, which shall be as prompt as possible. . . .

ARTICLE 5. Their Majesties . . . grant a full and
entire Amnesty to those of their subjects who may have
been compromised by any participation whatsoever in the

events of the War in favour of the cause of the enemy.

ARTICLE 7. [*Their Majesties*] declare the Sublime Porte admitted to participate in the advantages of the Public Law and System [*Concert*] of Europe. Their Majesties engage, each on his part, to respect the Independence and the Territorial Integrity of the Ottoman Empire; guarantee in common the strict observance of that engagement; and will, in consequence, consider any act tending to its violation as a question of general interest.

ARTICLE 8. If there should arise between the Sublime Porte and one or more of the other Signing Powers, any misunderstanding which might endanger the maintenance of their relations, the Sublime Porte, and each of such Powers, before having recourse to the use of force, shall afford to the other Contracting Parties the opportunity of preventing such an extremity by means of their Mediation.

ARTICLE 9. His Imperial Majesty the Sultan, having, in his constant solicitude for the welfare of his subjects, issued a Firman, which, while ameliorating their condition without distinction of Religion or of Race, records his generous intentions towards the Christian population of his Empire, and wishing to give a further proof of his sentiments in that respect, has resolved to communicate to the Contracting Parties the said Firman, emanating spontaneously from his Sovereign will.

The Contracting Parties recognize the high value of this communication. It is clearly understood that it cannot, in any case, give to the said Powers the right to interfere, either collectively or separately, in the relations of His Majesty the Sultan with his subjects, nor in the Internal Administration of his Empire.

ARTICLE 10. The Convention of the 13th of July, 1841, which maintains the ancient rule of the Ottoman Empire relative to the Closing of the Straits of the Bosporus and of the Dardanelles, has been revised by common consent.

The Act concluded for that purpose, and in conformity with that principle, between the High Contracting Parties, is and remains annexed to the present Treaty, and shall have the same force and validity as if it formed an integral part thereof.

ARTICLE 11. The Black Sea is Neutralized; its Waters and its Ports, thrown open to the Mercantile Marine of every Nation, are formally and in perpetuity interdicted to the Flag of War, either of the Powers possessing its Coasts, or of any other Power. . . .

ARTICLE 15. The Act of the Congress of Vienna, having established the principles intended to regulate the Navigation of Rivers which separate or traverse different States, the Contracting Parties stipulate among themselves that those principles shall in future be equally applied to the Danube and its Mouths. . . .

ARTICLE 16. With a view to carry out the arrangement of the preceding Article, a Commission, in which Great Britain, Austria, France, Prussia, Russia, Sardinia and Turkey, shall each be represented by one delegate, shall be charged to designate and to cause to be executed the Works necessary below Isatcha, to clear the Mouths of the Danube, as well as the neighbouring parts of the Sea, from the sands and other impediments which obstruct them, in order to put that part of the River and the said parts of the Sea in the best possible state for Navigation. . . .

ARTICLE 22. The Principalities of Wallachia and Moldavia shall continue to enjoy under the Suzerainty of the Porte, and under the Guarantee of the Contracting Powers, the Privileges and Immunities of which they are in possession. No exclusive Protection shall be exercised over them by any of the guaranteeing Powers.

There shall be no separate right of interference in their Internal Affairs.

ARTICLE 28. The Principality of Servia shall continue to hold of the Sublime Porte, in conformity with the Imperial Hats which fix and determine its Rights and Immunities, placed henceforward under the Collective Guarantee of the Contracting Powers. . . .

ARTICLE 34. The present Treaty shall be ratified, and the Ratifications shall be exchanged at Paris in the space of 4 weeks, or sooner if possible.

In witness whereof the respective Plenipotentiaries have signed the same, and have affixed thereto the Seal of their Arms.

Done at Paris, the 30th day of the month of March, in the year 1856.

> (L.S.) CLARENDON
> (L.S.) COWLEY
> (L.S.) BUOL-SCHAUENSTEIN
> (L.S.) HUBNER
> (L.S.) A. WALEWSKI
> (L.S.) BOURQUENEY
> (L.S.) MANTEUFFEL
> (L.S.) C. M. D'HATZFELDT
> (L.S.) ORLOFF
> (L.S.) BRUNNOW
> (L.S.) C. CAVOUR
> (L.S.) DE VILLAMARINA
> (L.S.) AALI
> (L.S.) MOHAMMED DJEMIL

— 24 —

JOHN STUART MILL'S ON LIBERTY 1859 [44]

The most complete and best expression of liberalism in the nineteenth century was made by John Stuart Mill (1806-1873), English philosopher and economist, in his famous essay, On Liberty. *Written in 1859, primarily as a challenge to the wave of reaction following the Revolutions of 1848,* On Liberty *summarized the faith of a liberal in the progress of mankind through freedom of thought. Every line vibrated with a spirit of faith in the ultimate triumph of liberalism. For Mill liberalism was a universal creed, not limited to class interests but ap-*

[44] John Stuart Mill, *On Liberty* (London, n.d.), pp. 17-26.

plicable to all of mankind. In clear-cut, logical terms he described the ideals of liberty, freedom of speech, liberty of association, and popular education. He denounced both individual and social tyranny.

Mills' famous essay was a source of inspiration to his contemporaries and to all those since his time who hold the liberal attitude. Because of the world's recent experiences with crippling totalitarianism, his plea for individual liberty has become even more compelling today. The following extracts from Mills' essay give the salient points of his argument.

✓   ✓   ✓

The object of this Essay is to assert one very simple principle, as entitled to govern absolutely the dealings of society with the individual in the way of compulsion and control, whether the means used be physical force in the form of legal penalties, or the moral coercion of public opinion. That principle is, that the sole end for which mankind are warranted, individually or collectively, in interfering with the liberty of action of any of their number; is self-protection. That the only purpose for which power can be rightfully exercised over any member of a civilised community, against his will, is to prevent harm to others. His own good, either physical or moral, is not a sufficient warrant. He cannot rightfully be compelled to do or forbear because it will be better for him to do so, because it will make him happier, because, in the opinion of others, to do so would be wise, or even right. These are good reasons for remonstrating with him, or reasoning with him, or persuading him, or entreating him, but not for compelling him, or visiting him with any evil in case he do otherwise. To justify that, the conduct from which it is desired to deter him must be calculated to produce evil to some one else. The only part of the conduct of any one, for which he is amenable to society, is that which concerns others. In the part which merely concerns himself, his independence is, of right, absolute. Over himself, over his own body and mind, the individual is sovereign.

It is, perhaps, hardly necessary to say that this doctrine is meant to apply only to human beings in the maturity of their faculties. We are not speaking of children, or of young persons below the age which the law may fix as that of manhood or womanhood. Those who are still in a state to require being taken care of by others, must be protected against their own actions as well as against external injury. For the same reason, we may leave out of consideration those backward states of society in which the race itself may be considered as in its nonage. The early difficulties in the way of spontaneous progress are so great, that there is seldom any choice of means for overcoming them; and a ruler so full of the spirit of improvement is warranted in the use of any expedients that will attain an end, perhaps otherwise unattainable. Despotism is a legitimate mode of government in dealing with barbarians, provided the end be their improvement, and the means justified by actually effecting that end. Liberty, as a principle, has no application to any state of things anterior to the time when mankind have become capable of being improved by free and equal discussion. Until then, there is nothing for them by implicit obedience to an Akbar or a Charlemagne, if they are so fortunate as to find one. But as soon as mankind have attained the capacity of being guided to their own improvement by conviction or persuasion (a period long since reached in all nations with whom we need here concern ourselves), compulsion, either in the direct form or in that of pains and penalties for non-compliance, is no longer admissible as a means to their own good, and justifiable only for the security of others.

It is proper to state that I forego any advantage which could be derived to my argument from the idea of abstract right, as a thing independent of utility. I regard utility as the ultimate appeal on all ethical questions; but it must be utility in the largest sense, grounded on the permanent interests of man as a progressive being. Those interests, I contend, authorise the subjection of individual spontaneity to external control, only in respect to those actions of each, which concern the interest of other people. If any one does an act hurtful to others, there is a *primâ facie* case for punishing him, by law, or, where legal penalties are not safely applicable, by general disapprobation. There are almost many positive acts for the benefit of others, which he may rightfully be compelled to perform; such as, to give evidence in a court of justice; to bear his fair share in the common defence, or in any other joint work necessary to the interest of the society of which he enjoys the protection; and to perform certain acts of individual beneficence, such as saving a fellow-creature's life, or interposing to protect the defenceless against ill-usage, things which whenever it is obviously a man's duty to do, he may rightfully be made responsible to society for not doing. A person may cause evil to others not only by his actions but by his inaction, and in either case he is justly accountable to them for the injury. The latter case, it is true, requires a much more cautious exercise of compulsion than the former. To make any one answerable for doing evil to others, is the rule; to make him answerable for not preventing evil, is, comparatively speaking, the exception. Yet there are many cases clear enough and grave enough to justify that exception. In all things which regard the external relations of the individual, he is *de jure* amenable to those whose interests are concerned, and if need be, to society as their protector. There are often good reasons for not holding him to the responsibility; but these reasons must arise from the special expediencies of the case: either because it is a kind of case in which he is on the whole likely to act better, when left to his own discretion, than when controlled in any way in which society have it in their power to control him; or because the attempt to exercise control would produce other evils, greater than those which it would prevent. When such reasons as these preclude the enforcement of responsibility, the conscience of the agent himself should step into the vacant judgment seat, and protect those interests of others which have no external protection; judging himself all the more rigidly, because the case does not admit of his being made accountable to the judgment of his fellow-creatures.

But there is a sphere of action in which society, as distinguished from the individual, has, if any, only an indirect interest; comprehending all that portion of a person's life and conduct which affects only himself, or if it also affects others, only with their free, voluntary, and undeceived consent and participation. When I say only himself, I mean directly, and in the first instance: for whatever affects himself, may affect others *through* himself; and the objection which may be grounded on this contingency, will receive consideration in the sequel. This, then, is the appropriate region of human liberty. It comprises, first, the inward domain of consciousness; demanding liberty of conscience, in the most comprehensive sense; liberty of thought and feeling; absolute freedom of opinion and sentiment on all subjects, practical or speculative, scientific, moral, or theological. The liberty of expressing and publishing opinions may seem to fall under a different principle, since it belongs to that part of the conduct of an individual which concerns other people; but, being almost of as much importance as the liberty of thought itself, and resting in part on the same reasons, it is practically inseparable from it. Secondly, the principle requires liberty of tastes and pursuits; of framing the plan of our life to suit our own character; of doing as we like, subject to such consequences as may follow: without impediment from our fellow-creatures, so long as what we do does not harm them, even though they should think our conduct foolish, perverse, or wrong. Thirdly, from this liberty of each individual, follows the liberty, within the same limits, of combination among individuals; freedom to unite, for any purpose not involving harm to others: the persons combining being supposed to be of full age, and not forced or deceived.

No society in which these liberties are not, on the whole, respected, is free, whatever may be its form of government; and none is completely free in which they do not exist absolute and unqualified. The only freedom which deserves the name, is that of pursuing our own good in our own way, so long as we do not attempt to deprive others of theirs, or impede their efforts to obtain it. Each is the proper guardian of his own health, whether bodily, or mental and spiritual. Mankind are greater gainers by suffering each other to live as seems good to themselves, than by compelling each to live as seems good to the rest.

Though this doctrine is anything but new, and, to some persons, may have the air of a truism, there is no doctrine which stands more directly opposed to the general tendency of existing opinion and practice. Society has expended fully as much effort in the attempt (according to its lights) to compel people to conform to its notions of personal, as of social excellence. The ancient commonwealths thought themselves entitled to practise, and the ancient philosophers countenanced, the regulation of every part of private conduct by public authority, on the ground that the State had a deep interest in the whole bodily and mental discipline of every one of its citizens; a mode of thinking which may have been admissible in small republics surrounded by powerful enemies, in constant peril of being subverted by foreign attack or internal commotion, and to which even a short interval of relaxed energy and self-command might so easily be fatal, that they could not afford to wait for the salutary permanent effects of freedom. In the modern world, the greater size of political communities, and above all, the separation between spiritual and temporal authority (which placed the direction of men's consciences in other hands than those which controlled their worldly affairs), prevented so great an interference by law in the details of private life; but the engines of moral repression have been wielded more strenuously against divergence from the reigning opinion in self-regarding, than even in social matters; religion, the most powerful of the elements which have entered into the formation of moral feeling, having almost always been governed either by the ambition of a hierarchy, seeking control over every department of human conduct, or by the spirit of Puritanism. And some of those modern reformers who have placed themselves in strongest opposition to the religions of the past, have been noway behind either churches or sects in their assertion of the right of spiritual domination: M. Comte, in particular, whose social system, as unfolded in his *Traité de Politique Positive,* aims at establishing (though by moral more than by legal appliances) a despotism of society over the individual, surpassing anything contemplated in the political ideal of the most rigid disciplinarian among the ancient philosophers.

Apart from the peculiar tenets of individual thinkers, there is also in the world at large an increasing inclination to stretch unduly the powers of society over the individual, both by the force of opinion and even by that of legislation: and as the tendency of all the changes taking place in the world is to strengthen society, and diminish the power of the individual, this encroachment is not one of the evils which tend spontaneously to disappear, but, on the contrary, to grow more and more formidable. The disposition of mankind, whether as rulers or as fellow-citizens, to impose their own opinions and inclinations as a rule of conduct on others, is so energetically supported by some of the best and by some of the worst feelings incident to human nature, that it is hardly ever kept under restraint by anything but want of power; and as the power is not declining, but growing, unless a strong barrier of moral conviction can be raised against the mischief, we must expect, in the present circumstances of the world, to see it increase.

— 25 —

CHARLES DARWIN AND THE THEORY OF EVOLUTION, SEPTEMBER 24, 1859

The most momentous event in the intellectual history of the nineteenth century was the publication on September 24, 1859 of The Origin of Species by Means of Natural Selection *by Charles Darwin (1809-1882), an English naturalist. Darwin and Alfred R. Wallace, another celebrated naturalist, arrived at similar ideas on evolution at approximately the same time. The first edition of Darwin's book, some 1,250 copies, was a first-day sell-out, an extraordinary publishing event at the time.*

In his famous book Darwin held that, because offspring can vary from parents and because nature tolerates only

*the survival of the fittest, the principle of natural selection
can explain the evolution of a high species from a low
one. The theory was of tremendous historical importance.*

*An important corollary of Darwinism in the nineteenth
century was Social Darwinism, which held that the
doctrine of natural selection in physical science should
be utilized not only for mere animal history, but, with a
change of form but an identical essence, should be applied
to human history. Thus, a scientific idea could be presented that those nations which are strongest should prevail over the others and that in certain marked peculiari-
ties the strongest tend to be the best.*

Following are extracts from Darwin's The Origin of
Species *and his later work,* The Descent of Man *(1871).*

✓   ✓   ✓

A

Extracts from the Introduction,
The Origin of Species *(1859)*[45]

When on board H.M.S. *'Beagle,'* as naturalist, I was
much struck with certain facts in the distribution of the
organic beings inhabiting South America, and in the geological relations of the present to the past inhabitants of
that continent. These facts . . . seemed to throw some
light on the origin of species—that mystery of mysteries,
as it has been called by our greatest philosophers. On my
return home, it occurred to me, in 1837, that something
might perhaps be made out of this question by patiently
accumulating and reflecting on all sorts of facts which
could possibly have any bearing on it. After five years'
work I allowed myself to speculate on the subject, and
drew up some short notes; these I enlarged in 1844 into
a sketch of the conclusions, which then seemed to me
probable: from that period to the present day I have
steadily pursued the same object. . . .

My work is now (1859) nearly finished; but it will take
me many more years to complete it, and as my health is
far from strong, I have been urged to publish this Ab-

[45] Charles Darwin, *The Origin of Species by Means of Natural Selection* (rev. ed., London, 1860), introduction,
passim.

stract. . . . This . . . must necessarily be imperfect. I cannot here give references and authorities for my several statements; and I must trust to the reader and authorities for my several statements. . . .

In considering the Origin of Species, it is quite conceivable that a naturalist, reflecting on the mutual affinities of organic beings, on their embryological relations, their geographical distribution, geological succession, and other such facts, might come to the conclusion that species had not been independently created, but had descended, like varieties, from other species. Nevertheless, such a conclusion, even if well founded, would be unsatisfactory, until it could be shown how the innumerable species inhabiting this world have been modified, so as to acquire that perfection of structure and coadaptation which justly excites our admiration. . . .

It is . . . of the highest importance to gain a clear insight into the means of modification and coadaptation. . . .

. . . I shall devote the first chapter of this Abstract to Variation under Domestication. We shall thus see that a large amount of hereditary modification is at least possible; and, what is equally or more important, we shall see how great is the power of man in acquiring by his Selection successive slight variations. . . . In the next chapter the Struggle for Existence amongst all organic beings throughout the world, which inevitably follows from the high geometrical ratio of their increase, will be considered. This is the doctrine of Malthus, applied to the whole animal and vegetable kingdoms. As many more individuals of each species are born than can possibly survive; and as, consequently, there is a frequently recurring struggle for existence, it follows that any being, if it vary however slightly in any manner profitable to itself, under the complex and sometimes varying conditions of life, will have a better chance of surviving, and thus be *naturally selected*. From the strong principle of inheritance, any selected variety will tend to propagate its new and modified form.

This fundamental subject of Natural Selection will be treated at some length in the fourth chapter; and we shall then see how Natural Selection almost inevitably causes much Extinction of the less improved forms of life, and leads to what I have called Divergence of Character. In the next chapter I shall discuss the complex and little known laws of variation. In the five succeeding chapters, the most apparent and gravest difficulties in accepting the theory will be given: namely, first, the difficulties of transition, or how a simple being or a simple organ can be changed and perfected into a highly developed being or into an elaborately constructed organ; secondly, the subject of Instinct, or the mental power of animals; thirdly, Hybridism, or the infertility of species and the fertility of varieties when intercrossed; and fourthly, the imperfection of the Geological Record. In the next chapter I shall consider the geological succession of organic beings throughout time; in the twelfth and thirteenth, their geographical distribution throughout space; in the fourteenth, their classification or mutual affinities, both when mature and in an embryonic condition. In the last chapter I shall give a brief recapitulation of the whole work, and a few concluding remarks.

B

Extracts from the Recapitulation and Conclusion,
The Origin of Species (*1859*)[46]

I see no good reason why the views given in this volume should shock the religious feelings of any one. It is satisfactory, as showing how transient such impressions are, to remember that the greatest discovery ever made by man, namely, the law of the attraction of gravity, was also attacked by Leibnitz, "as subversive of natural, and inferentially of revealed, religion." A celebrated author and divine has written to me that "he has gradually learnt to see that it is just as noble a conception of the Deity to believe that He created a few original forms capable of self-development into other and needful forms, as to believe that He required a fresh act of creation to supply the voids caused by the action of His laws." . . .

Authors of the highest eminence seem to be fully satisfied with the view that each species has been independently created. To my mind it accords better with what we know of the laws impressed on matter by the Creator,

[46] *Ibid.*, chap. 15, *passim.*

that the production and extinction of the past and present inhabitants of the world should have been due to secondary causes, like those determining the birth and death of the individual. When I view all beings not as special creations, but as the lineal descendants of some few beings which lived long before the first bed of the Cambrian system was deposited, they seem to me to become ennobled. . . .

It is interesting to contemplate a tangled bank, clothed with many plants of many kinds, with birds singing on the bushes, with various insects flitting about, and with worms crawling through the damp earth, and to reflect that these elaborately constructed forms, so different from each other, and dependent upon each other in so complex a manner, have all been produced by laws acting around us. These laws, taken in the largest sense, being Growth with Reproduction; Inheritance which is almost implied by reproduction; Variability from the indirect and direct action of the conditions of life, and from use and disuse: a Ratio of Increase so high as to lead to a Struggle for Life, and as a consequence to Natural Selection, entailing Divergence of Character and the Extinction of less-improved forms. Thus, from the war of nature, from famine and death, the most exalted object which we are capable of conceiving, namely, the production of the higher animals, directly follows. There is grandeur in this view of life, with its several powers, having been originally breathed by the Creator into a few forms or into one; and that, whilst this planet has gone cycling on according to the fixed law of gravity, from so simple a beginning endless forms most beautiful and most wonderful have been, and are being evolved.

C

Extract from the Conclusion of
The Descent of Man (1871)[47]

The main conclusion arrived at in this work, and now held by many naturalists who are well competent to form a sound judgment, is that man is descended from some

[47] Charles Darwin, The Descent of Man (London, 1871), II, 385-86.

less highly organized form. The grounds upon which this conclusion rests will never be shaken, for the close similarity between man and the lower animals in embryonic development, as well as in innumerable points of structure and constitution, both of high and of the most trifling importance—the rudiments which he retains, and the abnormal reversions to which he is occasionally liable—are facts which cannot be disputed. They have long been known, but until recently they told us nothing with respect to the origins of man. Now, when viewed by the light of our knowledge of the whole organic world, their meaning is unmistakable. The great principle of evolution stands up clear and firm, when these groups of facts are considered in connection with others, such as the mutual affinities of the members of the same group, their geographical distribution in past and present times, and their geological succession. It is incredible that all these facts should speak falsely. He who is not content to look, like a savage, at the phenomena of nature as disconnected, cannot any longer believe that man is the work of a separate act of creation. . . .

— 26 —

GARIBALDI AND THE UNIFICATION OF ITALY, MAY, 1860

While Count Cavour worked in the north of Italy on his major objective of driving Austria from Italian affairs, Giuseppe Garibaldi (1807-1882), a soldier of fortune and a leader of the Risorgimento *(Resurrection) was determined to settle accounts with the reactionary Neapolitan monarchy in the south. Assembling a motley force of 1062 Italians and five Hungarians, wearing*

*bright-red woolen shirts and red hats, the fiery, courage-
ous ex-candlestick maker set sail from Genoa on the
night of May 5, 1860, to invade the southern kingdom,
then under the despotism of Francis II. Luckily escap-
ing Neapolitan cruisers, the ragged band, after a month
of forced marches, sleepless nights, and exposure to
mountain rains and semitropical sun, entered Palermo
in triumph. After taking Sicily, Garibaldi sailed to
Naples, and at Volturno defeated an army twice the
size of his forces. Then, in November, 1860, he resigned,
sailed back to his farm on Caprera "with a large bag of
seed corn and a small handful of lira notes," and left
Victor Emmanuel the constitutional monarch of the new
kingdom of Italy.*

*The first document below gives Garibaldi's call to
arms before sailing on his mission. The second gives
extracts from the famous dispatch of the Hungarian-born
Nandor Eber, the London* Times *correspondent, on the
triumphal reception of Garibaldi in Palermo.*

✓   ✓   ✓

A

Garibaldi's Proclamation to the Italians, May 5, 1860 [48]

Italians!

The Sicilians are fighting against the enemies of Italy
and for Italy. To help them with money, arms, and especially men, is the duty of every Italian.

Let the Marches, Umbria, Sabine, the Roman Cam-
pagna, and the Neapolitan territory arise, so as to divide
the enemy's forces.

If the cities do not offer a sufficient basis for insur-
rection, let the more resolute throw themselves into the
open country.

In the name of Heaven, hearken not to the voice of
those who cram themselves at well-served tables.

Let us arm. Let us fight for our brothers; tomorrow
we can fight for ourselves.

A handful of brave men, who have followed me in
battles for our country, are advancing with me to the

[48] *Annual Register, 1860* (London, 1861), p. 221.

rescue. Italy knows them; they always appear at the hour of danger. Brave and generous companions, they have devoted their lives to their country; they will shed their last drop of blood for it, seeking no other reward than that of a pure conscience.

"Italy and Victor Emmanuel!"—that was our battle-cry when we crossed the Ticino; it will resound into the very depths of Aetna.

As this prophetic battle-cry re-echoes from the hills of Italy to the Tarpeian Mount, the tottering thrones of tyranny will fall to pieces, and the whole country will rise like one man.

B

Eber's Classic Report on the Reception of
Garibaldi in Palermo, May 31, 1860 [49]

PALERMO, MAY 31—Anyone in search of violent emotions cannot do better than set off at once for Palermo. However *blasé* he may be, or however milk-and-water his blood, I promise it will be stirred up. He will be carried away by the tide of popular feeling, or else the impetuosity and variation of this torrent will produce in him a reaction such as he rarely felt.

The popular proverb has it that no day resembles its predecessor. Here almost every hour changes the state of affairs, and with the state of affairs the feelings of 200,000 people change from one extreme to another almost without the slightest transition. . . .

In the afternoon Garibaldi made a tour of inspection round the town. I was there, but find it really impossible to give you a faint idea of the manner in which he was received everywhere. It was one of those triumphs which seem to be almost too much for a man. . . . The popular idol, Garibaldi, in his red flannel shirt, with a loose colored handkerchief round his neck, and his worn "wide-awake," [50] was walking on foot among those cheering, laughing, crying, mad thousands; and all his few followers could do was to prevent him from being bodily carried off the ground. The people threw themselves for-

[49] *The Times* (London), June 13, 1860.
[50] A soft-brimmed felt hat.

ward to kiss his hands, or, at least, to touch the hem of his garment, as if it contained the panacea for all their past and perhaps coming suffering. Children were brought up, and mothers asked on their knees for his blessing; and all this while the object of this idolatry was calm and smiling as when in the deadliest fire, taking up the children and kissing them, trying to quiet the crowd, stopping at every moment to hear a long complaint of houses burned and property sacked by the retreating soldiers, giving good advice, comforting, and promising that all damages should be paid for. . . .

One might write volumes of horrors on the vandalism already committed, for every one of the hundred ruins has its story of brutality and inhumanity. . . . In these small houses a dense population is crowded together even in ordinary times. The fear of bombardment crowded them even more. A shell falling on one, and crushing and burying the inmates, was sufficient to make people abandon the neighboring one and take refuge a little further on, shutting themselves up in the cellars. When the Royalists retired they set fire to those of the houses which had escaped the shells, and numbers were thus burned alive in their hiding places. . . .

If you can stand the exhalation, try and go inside the ruins, for it is only there that you will see what the thing means and you will not have to search long before you stumble over the remains of a human body, a leg sticking out here, an arm there, a black face staring at you a little further on. You are startled by a rustle. You look round and see half a dozen gorged rats scampering off in all directions, or you see a dog trying to make his escape over the ruins. . . .

I only wonder that the sight of these scenes does not convert every man in the town into a tiger and every woman into a fury. But these people have been so long ground down and demoralized that their nature seems to have lost the power of reaction.

THE IMPERIAL UKASE EMANCIPATING THE SERFS IN RUSSIA, MARCH 3, 1861 [51]

Serfdom, characteristic of the social order of the Middle Ages, had been entirely abolished in Western Europe by the French Revolution and Napoleon. But in the Russia of 1859 some 23,000,000 serfs were bound to the soil of such proprietors as the imperial family, the state, the Orthodox Church, and individual masters. "The present position," said Tsar Alexander II (1818-1881), "cannot last, and it is better to abolish serfdom from above than to wait until it begins to be abolished from below." A committee of officials and nobles, acting under the inspiration of the Tsar, drew up the Emancipation Law, which was issued as an ukáse, or imperial decree, on February 9 (March 3), 1861. By this decree the peasant became personally free at once, without any payment, and the proprietor was obliged to grant him his plot of land at a fixed rent with the eventual possibility of redeeming it at a price to be agreed upon later.

The proclamation of the Emancipation was undoubtedly the most important event in the history of Russia in the nineteenth century. It paved the way for other reforms as well as for the revolutionary movement that finally led to the destruction of tsarism.

✓   ✓   ✓

By the grace of God, we, Alexander II, Emperor and Autocrat of all the Russias, King of Poland, Grand Duke of Finland, etc., to all our faithful subjects, make known:

Called by Divine Providence and by the sacred right of inheritance to the throne of our ancestors, we took a vow in our innermost heart to respond to the mission

[51] *Annual Register, 1861*, pp. 207-12, *passim.*

which is intrusted to us as to surround with our affection and our Imperial solicitude all our faithful subjects of every rank and of every condition, from the warrior, who nobly bears arms for the defence of the country to the humble artisan devoted to the works of industry; from the official in the career of the high offices of the State to the laborer whose plough furrows the soil.

In considering the various classes and conditions of which the State is composed we came to the conviction that the legislation of the empire having wisely provided for the organization of the upper and middle classes and having defined with precision their obligations, their rights, and their privileges, has not attained the same degree of efficiency as regards the peasants attached to the soil, thus designated because either from ancient laws or from custom they have been hereditarily subjected to the authority of the proprietors, on whom it was incumbent at the same time to provide for their welfare. The rights of the proprietors have been hitherto very extended and very imperfectly defined by the law, which has been supplied by tradition, custom, and the good pleasure of the proprietors. . . .

These facts had already attracted the notice of our predecessors of glorious memory, and they had taken measures for improving the conditions of the peasants; but among those measures some were not stringent enough, insomuch that they remained subordinate to the spontaneous initiative of such proprietors who showed themselves animated with liberal intentions; and others, called forth by peculiar circumstances, have been restricted to certain localities or simply adopted as an experiment. It was thus that Alexander I published the regulation for the free cultivators, and that the late Emperor Nicholas, our beloved father, promulgated that one which concerns the peasants bound by contract. In the Western Governments regulations called "inventaires" had fixed the territorial allotments due to the peasants, as well as the amount of their rent dues; but all these reforms have only been applied in a very restricted manner.

We thus came to the conviction that the work of a serious improvement of the condition of the peasants was a sacred inheritance bequeathed to us by our ancestors, a mission which, in the course of events, Divine Providence called upon us to fulfil.

We have commenced this work by an expression of our Imperial confidence towards the nobility of Russia, which has given us so many proofs of its devotion to the Throne, and of its constant readiness to make sacrifices for the welfare of the country.

It is to the nobles themselves, conformable to their own wishes, that we have reserved the task of drawing up the propositions for the new organization of the peasants —propositions which make it incumbent upon them to limit their rights over the peasants, and to accept the onus of a reform which could not be accomplished without some material losses. Our confidence has not been deceived. We have seen the nobles assembled in committees in the districts, through the medium of their confidential agents, making the voluntary sacrifice of their rights as regards the personal servitude of the peasants. These committees, after having collected the necessary data, have formulated their propositions concerning the new organization of the peasants attached to the soil in their relations with the proprietors. . . .

In virtue of the new dispositions above mentioned, the peasants attached to the soil will be invested within a term fixed by the law with all the rights of free cultivators.

The proprietors retaining their rights of property on all the land belonging to them, grant to the peasants for a fixed regulated rental the full enjoyment of their close; and, moreover, to assure their livelihood and to guarantee the fulfilment of their obligations towards the Government, the quantity of arable land is fixed by the said dispositions, as well as other rural appurtenances.

But, in the enjoyment of these territorial allotments, the peasants are obliged, in return, to acquit the rentals fixed by the same dispositions to the profit of the proprietors. In this state, which must be a transitory one, the peasants shall be designated as "temporary bound."

At the same time, they are granted the right of purchasing their close, and, with the consent of the proprietors, they may acquire in full property the arable lands and other appurtenances which are allotted to them as a permanent holding. By the acquisition in full property of the quantity of land fixed, the peasants are free from their obligations towards the proprietors for land thus purchased, and they enter definitely into the condition of free peasants—landholders. . . .

And now, pious and faithful people, make upon the forehead the sacred sign of the cross, and join thy prayers to ours to call down the blessing of the Most High upon thy first free labors, the sure pledge of thy personal well-being and of the public prosperity.

Given at St. Petersburg, the 19th day of February (March 3), of the year of Grace 1861, and the seventh of our reign.

ALEXANDER

— 28 —

BISMARCK'S "IRON AND BLOOD" SPEECH, SEPTEMBER 30, 1862 [52]

The Prussian elections of 1862 resulted in an over-whelming victory for the Liberals. William I, who had succeeded to the throne a year earlier, was determined to introduce universal conscription as a means of dou-bling the military forces of the nation. The Landtag promptly defeated the army budget. Depressed and con-templating abdication, William was persuaded by his Minister of War, Albrecht von Roon, to appoint Bis-marck provisional Minister-President of Prussia.

On September 30, 1862, Bismarck appeared before some thirty members of the Budget Commission of the

[52] Horst Kohl, ed., *Die politischen Reden des Fürsten Bis-marcks: historische-kritische Gesammtausgabe* (14 vols.; Stuttgart, 1892-1904), II, 29-30.

*Lower House of the Prussian Parliament and attempted
to persuade it to vote for the army increases desired by
the king. The new minister spoke with wit and incisive-
ness. He warned his listeners not to exaggerate their
powers. The Prussian Constitution, he said, did not give
the Lower House the sole power of settling the budget;
it must be settled by arrangement with the other House
and the Crown. He ended his conversational speech with
the famous "iron and blood" phrase given in the extract
below.*

*There was no verbatim report of Bismarck's speech,
but his words soon ran like wildfire all over Germany,
with the rhythm of the phrase changed to "blood and
iron." Despite criticism at home and abroad, Bismarck
never repudiated his words, although he did try to explain that all he meant by the word "blood" was "soldiers."*

The Landtag *refused to grant the requested war
credits, whereupon Bismarck, in defiance of the Constitution of 1850, and on the ground that "necessity alone
is authoritative," proceeded to levy, collect, and spend
taxes without presenting a budget or accounting. In 1866,
following the defeat of Austria in the Seven Weeks' War,
the Prussian parliament passed an act of indemnity retro-
actively legalizing Bismarck's actions in governing without a budget. But the shadow of 1862 influenced the
entire subsequent course of German history.*

✓   *✓*   *✓*

It is true that we can hardly escape complications in
Germany, although we do not seek them. Germany does
not look to Prussia's liberalism, but to her power.
The South German States—Bavaria, Württemberg, and
Baden, would like to indulge in liberalism, and because
of that no one will assign Prussia's rôle to them ! Prussia
must collect her forces and hold them in reserve for
an opportune moment, which has already come and gone
several times. Since the Treaty of Vienna, our frontiers
have not been favorably designed for a healthy body
politic. Not by speeches and majorities will the great
questions of the day be decided—that was the mistake
of 1848 and 1849—but by iron and blood.

29

THE EMANCIPATION PROCLAMATION, JANUARY 1, 1863

Early in the Civil War the extreme Republicans urged that measures be taken to destroy slavery. On July 22, 1862, Lincoln read to his cabinet a tentative emancipation proclamation to apply to the seceding states, but Secretary of State Seward urged that the announcement wait until the army won a victory, otherwise the proclamation would be construed as "the government stretching forth its hands to Ethiopia." The opponents of slavery, unaware of this secret action of the cabinet, continued to attack the President. On August 20, Horace Greeley, editor of the New York Tribune, wrote an editorial entitled, "The Prayer of Twenty Millions," in which he castigated Lincoln for his slowness in announcing emancipation. The President replied: "My paramount object in this struggle is to save the Union, and is not to save or destroy slavery. If I could save the Union without freeing any slave, I would do it; and if I could save it by freeing all the slaves, I would do it; and if I could save it by freeing some and leaving others alone, I would also do that."

A Preliminary Emancipation Proclamation (September 22, 1862) was followed by the Emancipation Proclamation (January 1, 1863), which declared that all slaves in areas still in rebellion were "then, thenceforward, and forever free." The Proclamation had no basis in the law of civil affairs, but Lincoln held it to be within his authority to issue it as commander-in-chief of the army and navy. Actually, the Proclamation freed no slaves; it went no further than Congress had already gone in legislation on the matter, since it applied only to areas over which the Federal government had no control. But, as the culminating point of the long struggle over the question of slavery, the Proclamation turned out to be the most significant act of Lincoln's administration.

✔   ✔   ✔

A

The Emancipation Proclamation, January 1, 1863 [53]

BY THE PRESIDENT OF THE UNITED STATES OF AMERICA:

A Proclamation

Whereas on the 22d day of September, A.D. 1862, a proclamation was issued by the President of the United States, containing, among other things, the following, to wit:

"That on the 1st day of January, A.D. 1863, all persons held as slaves within any State or designated part of a State the people whereof shall then be in rebellion against the United States shall be then, thenceforward, and forever free; and the executive government of the United States, including the military and naval authority thereof, shall recognize and maintain the freedom of such persons and will do no act or acts to repress such persons, or any of them, in any efforts they may make for their actual freedom.

"That the executive will on the 1st day of January aforesaid, by proclamation, designate the States and parts of States, if any, in which the people thereof, respectively, shall then be in rebellion against the United States; and the fact that any State or the people thereof shall on that day be in good faith represented in the Congress of the United States by members chosen thereto at elections wherein a majority of the qualified voters of such States shall have participated shall, in the absence of strong counterprevailing testimony, be deemed conclusive evidence that such State and the people thereof are not then in rebellion against the United States."

Now, therefore, I, Abraham Lincoln, President of the United States, by virtue of the power in me vested as

[53] *U.S. Statutes at Large,* XII, 1268-69.

Commander-in-Chief of the Army and Navy of the United States in time of actual armed rebellion against the authority and government of the United States, and as a fit and necessary war measure for suppressing such rebellion, do, on this 1st day of January, A.D. 1863, and in accordance with my purpose to do so, publicly proclaimed for the full period of one hundred days from the first day above mentioned, order and designate as the States and parts of States wherein the people thereof, respectively, are this day in rebellion against the United States the following, to wit:

Arkansas, Texas, Louisiana (except the parishes of St. Bernard, Plaquemines, Jefferson, St. John, St. Charles, St. James, Ascension, Assumption, Terrebonne, Lafourche, St. Mary, St. Martin, and Orleans, including the city of New Orleans), Mississippi, Alabama, Florida, Georgia, South Carolina, North Carolina, and Virginia (except the forty-eight counties designated as West Virginia, and also the counties of Berkeley, Accomac, Northampton, Elizabeth City, York, Princess Anne, and Norfolk, including the cities of Norfolk and Portsmouth), and which excepted parts are for the present left precisely as if this proclamation were not issued.

And by virtue of the power for the purpose aforesaid, I do order and declare that all persons held as slaves within said designated States and parts of States are, and henceforward shall be, free; and that the Executive Government of the United States, including the military and naval authorities thereof, will recognize and maintain the freedom of said persons.

And I hereby enjoin upon the people so declared to be free to abstain from all violence, unless in necessary self-defense; and I recommend to them that, in all cases when allowed, they labor faithfully for reasonable wages.

And I further declare and make known that such persons of suitable condition will be received into the armed forces of the United States to garrison forts, positions, stations, and other places, and to man vessels of all sorts in said service.

And upon this act, sincerely believed to be an act of justice, warranted by the Constitution upon military necessity, I invoke the considerate judgment of mankind and the gracious favor of Almighty God.

B

Handbill Distributed in Winchester, Virginia, January 5, 1863 [54]

FREEDOM TO SLAVES!

Whereas, the President of the United States did, on the first day of the present month, issue his *Proclamation* declaring that *"all persons held as Slaves in certain designated States, and parts of States, are, and henceforward shall be free,"* and that the Executive Government of the United States, including the Military and Naval authorities thereof, would recognize and maintain the freedom of said persons. *And Whereas,* the county of *Frederick* is included in the territory designated by the Proclamation of the President, in which the *Slaves should become free,* I therefore hereby notify the citizens of the city of Winchester, and of said County, of said Proclamation, and of my intention to maintain and enforce the same.

I expect all citizens to yield a ready compliance with the Proclamation of the Chief Executive, and I admonish all persons disposed to resist its peaceful enforcement, that upon manifesting such disposition by acts, they will be regarded as rebels in arms against the lawful authority of the Federal Government and dealt with accordingly.

All persons liberated by said Proclamation are admonished to abstain from all violence, and immediately betake themselves to useful occupations.

The officers of this command are admonished and ordered to act in accordance with said proclamation and to yield their ready co-operation in its enforcement.

R. H. MILROY
Brig. Gen'l Commanding

Jan. 5th, 1863

[54] This was the type of handbill used by the Union forces in psychological warfare after the Emancipation Proclamation was issued.

30

THE PAPAL *SYLLABUS OF ERRORS*, DECEMBER 8, 1864 [55]

Pope Pius IX (1846-1878) conducted a vigorous campaign against what he called "the errors of modern society and thought." His series of criticisms of the influence of modernism on ecclesiastical life culminated in the famous encyclical Quanta Cura *and the accompanying* Syllabus of Errors, *published on December 8, 1864. The encyclical condemned liberalism, individualism, and secularism, and upheld the earlier ideal of the Christian State. The* Syllabus *gave all the doctrines that had received papal condemnation and specifically castigated freethinkers, agnostics, materialists, naturalists, anti-clericals, nationalists, liberals, Freemasons, and "indifferent" persons. Pius claimed for the Church the control of culture, science, and education, while rejecting liberty of faith, conscience, and worship for other creeds.*

In effect, the Syllabus *declared war on modern society and committed the papacy to the principles of Ultramontanism. It was bitterly criticized on the ground that "Rome has refurbished and paraded anew every rusty tool she was fondly thought to have disused." Catholic circles belittled the significance of the manifesto and pointed out that it was issued not as ecclesiastical dogma (it was compiled by a committee of cardinals and was not signed by the Pope personally), but rather as counsel against the "abuses" of modern liberalism. However, its translator, Cardinal Manning, Archbishop of Westminster, declared it to be an emanation from the highest doctrinal authority in the Church, and the next Pope, Leo XIII, re-stated its major principles.*

The following extracts from the Syllabus *give the more important errors as listed in the document. It will*

[55] W. E. Gladstone, *The Vatican Decrees* (New York and London, 1875), pp. 110-29.

be noted that the clauses are purely negative, and that the Church enjoined the opposite of what it condemned as error.

✓ ✓ ✓

The Syllabus of the principal errors of our time, which are stigmatized in the Consistorial Allocutions, Encyclicals, and other Apostolical Letters of our Most Holy Father, Pope Pius IX

I. Pantheism, Naturalism, and Absolute Rationalism

1. There exists no supreme, most wise, and most provident divine being distinct from the universe, and God is none other than nature, and is therefore subject to change. In effect, God is produced in man and in the world, and all things are God, and have the very substance of God. God is therefore one and the same thing with the world, and thence spirit is the same thing with matter, necessity with liberty, true with false, good with evil, justice with injustice.

2. All action of God upon man and the world is to be denied.

3. Human reason, without any regard to God, is the sole arbiter of truth and falsehood, of good and evil; it is its own law to itself, and suffices by its natural force to secure the welfare of men and of nations.

4. All the truths of religions are derived from the native strength of human reason; whence reason is the master rule by which man can and ought to arrive at the knowledge of all truths of every kind.

6. Christian faith contradicts human reason, and divine revelation not only does not benefit, but even injures the perfection of man.

II. Modern Rationalism

8. As human reason is placed on a level with religion, so theological matters must be treated in the same manner as philosophical ones.

9. All the dogmas of the Christian religion are, without exception, the object of scientific knowledge or

philosophy, and human reason, instructed solely by history, is able, by its own natural strength and principles, to arrive at the true knowledge of even the most abstruse dogmas: provided such dogmas be proposed as subject-matter for human reason.

12. The decrees of the Apostolic See and the Roman Congregations fetter the true progress of science.

13. The method and principles by which the old scholastic doctors cultivated theology are no longer suitable to the demands of the age and the progress of science.

14. Philosophy must be treated of without any account being taken of supernatural revelation.

III. Indifferentism, Latitudinarianism

15. Every man is free to embrace and profess the religion he shall believe true, guided by the light of reason.

18. Protestantism is nothing more than another form of the same true Christian religion, in which it is possible to be equally pleasing to God as in the Catholic Church.

V. Errors concerning the Church and Her Rights

19. The Church is not a true, and perfect, and entirely free society, nor does she enjoy peculiar and perpetual rights conferred on her by her Divine Founder, but it appertains to the civil power to define what are the rights and limits with which the Church may exercise authority.

20. The ecclesiastical power must not exercise its authority without the permission and assent of the civil government.

VI. Errors about Civil Society, Considered Both in Itself and in its Relation to the Church

42. In the case of conflicting laws between the two powers, the civil law ought to prevail.

44. The civil authority may interfere in matters relating to religion, morality, and spiritual government.

Hence it has control over the instructions for the guidance of consciences issued, conformably with their mission, by the pastors of the Church. Further, it possesses power to decree, in the matter of administering the divine sacraments, as to the dispositions necessary for their reception.

47. The best theory of civil society requires that popular schools open to the children of all classes, and, generally, all public institutes intended for instruction in letters and philosophy, and for conducting the education of the young, should be freed from all ecclesiastical authority, government, and interference, and should be fully subject to the civil and political power, in conformity with the will of rulers and the prevalent opinions of the age.

55. The Church ought to be separated from the State, and the State from the Church.

VII. Errors concerning Natural and Christian Ethics

56. Moral laws do not stand in need of the divine sanction, and there is no necessity that human laws should be conformable to the laws of nature, and receive their sanction from God.

VIII. The Errors concerning Christian Marriage

66. The sacrament of marriage is only an adjunct of the contract, and separable from it, and the sacrament itself consists in the nuptial benediction alone.

73. A merely civil contract may, among Christians, constitute a true marriage; and it is false, either that the marriage contract between Christians is always a sacrament, or that the contract is null if the sacrament be excluded.

IX. Errors regarding the Civil Power of the Sovereign Pontiff

76. The abolition of the temporal power, of which the Apostolic See is possessed, would contribute in the greatest degree to the liberty and prosperity of the Church.

X. Errors having reference to
Modern Liberalism

77. In the present day, it is no longer expedient that the Catholic religion shall be held as the only religion of the State, to the exclusion of all other modes of worship.

78. Whence it has been wisely provided by law, in some countries called Catholic, that persons coming to reside therein shall enjoy the public exercise of their own worship.

79. Moreover, it is false that the civil liberty of every mode of worship, and the full power given to all of overtly and publicly manifesting their opinions and their ideas, of all kinds whatsoever, conduce more easily to corrupt the morals and minds of the people, and to the propagation of the pest of indifferentism.

80. The Roman Pontiff can and ought to reconcile himself to, and agree with, progress, liberalism, and civilization as lately introduced.

— 31 —

LINCOLN'S SECOND INAUGURAL ADDRESS, MARCH 4, 1865 [56]

In the presidential elections of November 8, 1864, Lincoln was reëlected by 212 electoral votes to McClellan's 21, but with a popular majority of but 400,000 out of 4 million votes. In his second inaugural address, de-

[56] James D. Richardson, ed., *Compilation of the Messages and Papers of the Presidents, 1789-1897* (Washington, 1896-99), VI, 276 ff.

livered on March 4, 1865, Lincoln spoke in inspired words on the profound moral significance of the war which he now saw drawing to a close. He appealed to the people to forget vengeance, to bind up the nation's wounds, and to do everything to achieve a just and lasting peace. Less than six weeks later the great President fell victim to the assassin, John Wilkes Booth.

↗   ↗   ↗

FELLOW-COUNTRYMEN:—At this second appearing to take the oath of the presidential office there is less occasion for an extended address than there was at the first. Then a statement somewhat in detail of a course to be pursued seemed fitting and proper. Now, at the expiration of four years, during which public declarations have been constantly called forth on every point and phase of the great contest which still absorbs the attention and engrosses the energies of the nation, little that is new could be presented. The progress of our arms, upon which all else chiefly depends, is as well known to the public as to myself, and it is, I trust, reasonably satisfactory and encouraging to all. With high hope for the future, no prediction in regard to it is ventured.

On the occasion corresponding to this four years ago all thoughts were anxiously directed to an impending civil war. All dreaded it, all sought to avert it. While the inaugural address was being delivered from this place, devoted altogether to *saving* the Union without war, insurgent agents were in the city seeking to *destroy* it without war—seeking to dissolve the Union and divide effects by negotiation. Both parties deprecated war, but one of them would *make* war rather than let the nation survive, and the other would *accept* war rather then let it perish, and the war came.

One eighth of the whole population was colored slaves, not distributed generally over the Union, but localized in the southern part of it. These slaves constituted a peculiar and powerful interest. All knew that this interest was somehow the cause of the war. To strengthen, perpetuate, and extend this interest was the object for which the insurgents would rend the Union even by war, while the Government claimed no right to do more than to restrict the territorial enlargement of it. Neither party expected for the war the magnitude or the duration which it has already attained. Neither anticipated that the *cause* of the conflict might cease with or even before the conflict itself should cease. Each looked for an easier triumph, and a result less fundamental and astounding. Both read the same Bible and prayed to the same God, and each invokes His aid against the other. It may seem strange that any men should dare to ask a just God's assistance in wringing their bread from the sweat of other men's faces, but let us judge not, that we be not judged. The prayers of both could not be answered. That of neither has been answered fully. The Almighty has His own purposes. "Woe unto the world because of offenses; for it must needs be that offenses come, but woe to that man by whom the offense cometh." If we shall suppose that American slavery is one of those offenses which, in the providence of God, must needs come, but which, having continued through His appointed time, He now wills to remove, and that He gives to both North and South this terrible war as the woe due to those by whom the offense came, shall we discern therein any departure from those divine attributes which the believers in a living God always ascribe to Him? Fondly do we hope, fervently do we pray, that this mighty scourge of war may speedily pass away. Yet, if God wills that it continue until all the wealth piled by the bondsman's two hundred and fifty years of unrequited toil shall be sunk, and until every drop of blood drawn with the lash shall be paid by another drawn with the sword, as was said three thousand years ago, so still it must be said, "The judgments of the Lord are true and righteous altogether."

With malice toward none, with charity for all, with firmness in the right as God gives us to see the right, let us strive on to finish the work we are in, to bind up the nation's wounds, to care for him who shall have borne the battle and for his widow and his orphan, to do all which may achieve and cherish a just and lasting peace among ourselves and with all nations.

THE AUSTRO-PRUSSIAN WAR, 1866

In 1850, Frederick William IV attempted to unify Germany by negotiating directly with the other princes. Austria, promptly summoned him to Olmütz, a small town in Austria, and ordered him immediately to abandon his plan.

The "humiliation" of Olmütz rankled deeply in the breasts of Prussian patriots. Bismarck, especially, was determined to remove Austria in one way or another as an obstacle to German unification. With characteristic shrewdness, he isolated Austria from foreign help: he promised Venetia to the newly formed Kingdom of Italy for assistance in a possible war against Austria; at Biarritz he succeeded in gaining Napoleon III's inactivity by vague promises to allow France to annex Belgium; and, in 1863, he had signed a convention with Russia promising Prussia's assistance in suppressing the Poles.

Bismarck cleverly utilized the complications involved in the disposal of Schleswig-Holstein to bring the issue to a head. In June, 1866, he accused the Austrian governor of Holstein of breaking the agreement of joint administration. Furthermore, he demanded that the Bundestag vote to apply federal sanctions against Austria on the ground that she had violated the principles upon which the union of 1815 was founded. Several days later, on June 18, 1866, King William issued a proclamation to the German people, which is reprinted here.

There has been much dispute among historians as to whether or not Bismarck's intention was from the beginning to make war against Austria. In a recent opinion, Erich Eyck wrote: "[Bismarck] certainly never had any scruples about a war of this kind, which he himself in later years called 'fraternal.' But it is another question whether he wanted the war. The answer is that he would have been willing to do without the war if he

*had been able to achieve his aims by normal diplomatic
means. . . . Thus the conclusion may be reached that,
although Bismarck was not from the beginning bent on
war with Austria, he was engaged in a policy which
made war unavoidable."* [57]

✓   ✓   ✓

A

William I's Summons to the Prussian People:
"An mein Volk," *June 18, 1866* [58]

I am moved to address my people at the moment when
the army of Prussia is advancing to a decisive battle.
I speak to the sons and grandsons of those courageous
forefathers to whom a half a century ago my father
(now resting in God) uttered the never-to-be-forgotten
words: "The country is in danger!" Austria and a great
part of Germany are now armed against us.

It has been but a few years since, when there was a
problem of liberating a German land from foreign domination, I voluntarily, and without thinking of any
previous differences of opinion, extended the hand of
friendship to the emperor of Austria. I had hoped that,
out of the blood shed in common on the field of battle,
a brotherhood in arms would have emerged that might
in turn lead to a stronger union based on mutual respect
and gratefulness. I believed that this would bring with
it that coöperation that should have as its first result
the domestic welfare of Germany and the enhancement
of her prestige among the nations.

However, this hope has been frustrated. Austria cannot forget that its princes once governed Germany. In
the younger but powerfully developing Prussia, she re-
fuses to see a natural ally, but only a hostile rival.
Austria reasons that Prussia must be opposed on every
occasion, on the ground that what is good for Prussia
is bad for Austria. The old, unhappy jealousy has blazed
up once more. Prussia is to be weakened, annihilated,
dishonored. No treaties are to be observed with Prussia;

[57] Erich Eyck, *Bismarck and the German Empire* (London,
1950), pp. 125, 126-27.
[58] M. Schilling, *Quellenbuch zur Geschichte der Neuzeit* (Berlin, 1884), pp. 456-57.

the confederated princes have not only been aroused against Prussia, but they have been also induced to dissolve the union. Wherever we look through Prussia, there we are surrounded by enemies, who cry "Down with Prussia!"

But the spirit of 1813 still lives in my people. No one can rob us of one foot of Prussian soil, if we are strongly determined to protect the land acquired by our fathers; if King and his people are united more firmly than ever before by the danger to the Fatherland; and if they hold it to be their highest and most sacred duty to risk their blood and possessions for her honor. In anxious expectation of what has now occurred, I have for many years regarded it as the prime duty of my royal office to prepare Prussia's military resources for a powerful show of strength. No Prussian can fail to look, even as I now do, with confidence and satisfaction upon the military forces which protect our boundaries. With their King at their head, the Prussian people, in truth, feel themselves to be a nation in arms. Our enemies are fooling themselves if they dream that Prussia is paralyzed by domestic discord. Against any enemy this nation is a single powerful unit. All differences dissolve in the face of the enemy, and we stand united, for good or for ill.

I have done all that I could possibly do to spare Prussia the burden and sacrifices of a war. My people are aware of this. God, who searches all hearts, knows it. To the very last moment, I have, in combination with France, England, and Russia, attempted to keep open the path to a peaceful settlement. Austria, however, was opposed to this. . . .

Let us pray to Almighty God, the director of the history of all nations, the disposer of battles, to bless our arms. Should He give us victory, then we shall be strong enough to renew, in a firmer and more beneficent manner, the bonds which have loosely bound the German lands together, in name rather than in fact, and which have now been torn apart by those who fear the right and might of the national spirit.

May God be with us!

Berlin, June 18, 1866   WILLIAM

B

Extracts from the Treaty of Prague, August 23, 1866 [59]

In the name of the All Highest and Indivisible Trinity!

His Majesty, the King of Prussia, and His Majesty, the Emperor of Austria, animated by the desire to bring back to their countries the benefits of peace, have agreed to transform the preliminary negotiations signed at Nikolsburg on July 26, 1866 into a definite treaty of peace. . . .

ARTICLE 2. As a means of implementing Article 6 of the peace preliminaries, . . . His Majesty, the Emperor of Austria, agrees to the union of the Kingdom of Lombardy-Venetia and the Kingdom of Italy, without any other burdensome conditions. . . .

ARTICLE 4. His Majesty, the Emperor of Austria, recognizes the dissolution of the former German Bund and gives his assent to a new form of Germany without participation of the Austrian Empire. . . .

ARTICLE 5. His Majesty, the Emperor of Austria, assigns to His Majesty, the King of Prussia, all the rights acquired by the Vienna Peace of October 30, 1864 in the Duchies of Holstein and Schleswig, with the added understanding, that the population of the northern district of Schleswig, if they have expressed the wish through a free plebiscite to enter a union with Denmark, shall be transferred to Denmark. . . .

ARTICLE 11. His Majesty, the Emperor of Austria, pledges himself, in order to help cover a part of the war costs of Prussia, to pay to His Majesty, the King of Prussia, the sum of forty million Prussian thalers. From this sum there will be subtracted fifteen million Prussian thalers, which Austria, according to Article 12 of the Vienna Peace of October 30, 1864, is still to receive from the Duchies of Schleswig and Holstein, and an additional five million Prussian thalers, as equivalent for the costs of the Prussian army in Austria during the occupation until the conclusion of peace, so that only

[59] Aegidi and Klauhold, *Das Staatsarchiv* (Hamburg, 1861 ff.), XI, 176 ff.

twenty million Prussian thalers remain to be paid in cash.

Half of this sum is to be paid concurrently with the exchange of ratifications of the present treaty, and the second half to be paid in cash three weeks later. . . .

ARTICLE 14. The ratification of the present treaty shall be exchanged at Prague within the space of eight days, or sooner if possible.

In witness whereof the respective plenipotentiaries have signed the present treaty, and have affixed to it the seals of their arms.

Done at Prague, on the 23rd day of the month of August, in the year of Grace, 1866.

(L.S.) BRENNER (L.S.) WERTHER

— 33 —

THE BRITISH NORTH AMERICA ACT, JULY 1, 1867[60]

In 1791, Upper Canada, which was dominantly English in population and sentiment, was separated from Lower Canada, which was overwhelmingly French. Friction between the two royal governors and the two popularly elected constitutional bodies led to rebellions in both provinces (1837-38). Lord Durham, sent over by England with authority to crush the insurrections, issued a report in 1839, since called "the Magna Carta of the colonies," recommending the union of the two Canadian provinces at once, the ultimate union of all British North America, and the granting of full self-government. This Report, which obviously took into account British experi-

[60] *Public General Statutes,* II, 5 ff., 30 Victoria, c. 3.

ence in the American Revolution, was a masterly survey that profoundly influenced the subsequent history of Canada.

In 1867 the British North America Act united Canada, Nova Scotia, and New Brunswick to form the Dominion of Canada, and divided Canada into four provinces—Ontario, Nova Scotia, New Brunswick, and Quebec. During the subsequent westward expansion, additional provinces and territories not under its control in 1867 were admitted to the Confederation.

✓   ✓   ✓

An act for the union of Canada, Nova Scotia, and New Brunswick, and the government thereof, and for purposes connected therewith. Whereas the provinces of Canada, Nova Scotia, and New Brunswick have expressed their desire to be federally united into one dominion under the crown of the united kingdom of Great Britain and Ireland, with a constitution similar in principle to that of the united kingdom; and whereas such a union would conduce to the welfare of the provinces and promote the interests of the British Empire; and whereas, on the establishment of the union by authority of parliament, it is expedient, not only that the constitution of the legislative authority in the dominion be provided for, but also that the nature of the executive government therein be declared; and whereas it is expedient that provision be made for the eventual admission into the union of other parts of British North America: be it therefore enacted. . . .

1. *Preliminary.* This act may be cited as the British North America Act, 1867. The provisions of the act referring to her majesty the queen extend also to the heirs and successors of her majesty, kings and queens of the united kingdom of Great Britain and Ireland.

2. *Union.* It shall be lawful for the queen, by and with the advice of her majesty's most honourable privy council, to declare by proclamation that on and after a day therein appointed, not being more than six months after the passing of this act, the provinces of Canada, Nova Scotia, and New Brunswick shall form and be one dominion under the name of Canada; and on and after that day those three provinces shall form and be one dominion

under that name. . . . Canada shall be divided into four
provinces: named Ontario, Quebec, Nova Scotia, and New
Brunswick. . . .

3. *Executive Power*. The executive government and authority of and over Canada is hereby declared to continue
and be vested in the queen. . . .

There shall be a council to aid and advise in the government of Canada, to be styled the queen's privy council for
Canada; and the persons who are to be members of that
council shall be from time to tie chosen and summoned by
the governor general. . . .

All powers, authorities, and functions . . . vested in or
exercisable by the respective governors or lieutenant governors . . . shall . . . be vested in and exercisable by the
governor general with the advice, or with the advice and
consent of, or in conjunction with the queen's privy council for Canada. . . .

The command-in-chief of the land and naval militia, and
of all naval and military forces of and in Canada, is hereby
declared to continue and be vested in the queen.

4. *Legislative Power*. There shall be one parliament for
Canada, consisting of the queen, and upper house styled
the senate, and the house of commons. . . .

The senate shall . . . consist of seventy-two members
who shall be styled senators. . . . The qualifications of a
senator shall be as follows: (1) He shall be of the full age
of thirty years; (2) He shall be either a natural-born subject of the queen naturalized by an act of the parliament of
Great Britain; . . . (3) He shall be legally or equitably
seised as of freehold for his own use and benefit of lands
or tenements . . . within the province for which he is appointed of the value of $4000 over and above all rents,
dues, debts, charges, mortgages, and incumbrances; (4)
His real and personal property shall be together worth
$4000 over and above his debts and liabilities; (5) He shall
be resident in the province for which he is appointed. . . .

The house of commons shall . . . consist of 181 members, of whom 82 shall be elected for Ontario, 65 for Quebec, 19 for Nova Scotia, and 15 for New Brunswick. . . .

Bills for appropriating any part of the public revenue,
or for imposing any tax or impost, shall originate in the
house of commons. . . .

Where a bill passed by the houses of the parliament is presented to the governor general for the queen's assent, he shall declare, according to his discretion . . . either that he assents thereto, or that he reserves the bill for the signification of the queen's pleasure. . . .

5. *Provincial Constitutions.* For each province there shall be an officer styled the lieutenant governor, appointed by the governor general in council by instrument under the great seal of Canada. . . .

6. *Distribution of Legislative Powers.* It shall be lawful for the queen, by and with the advice and consent of the senate and house of commons, to make laws for the peace, order, and good government of Canada in relation to all matters not coming within the classes of subjects by this act assigned exclusively to the legislatures of the provinces. . . .

7. *Judicature.* The governor general shall appoint the judges of the superior, district, and county courts in each province, except those of the courts of probate in Nova Scotia and New Brunswick. . . .

— 34 —

THE FORSTER ELEMENTARY EDUCATION ACT, 1870[61]

For the better part of the nineteenth century, elementary educational facilities in England were much inferior to those on the Continent. In the year 1870 there were accommodations in inspected day schools for about 2,000,-000 children; the average attendance was about 1,168,000. There were, with the exception of the well-to-do classes,

[61] *Public General Statutes,* V, 443 ff., 33-34 Victoria, c. 75.

some 1,500,000 children who attended no school at all or schools not under inspection.

Under the stimulus of William Edward Forster (1818-1886), the Gladstone administration in 1870 undertook a comprehensive measure of educational reform. The Elementary Education Act, introduced on February 17, 1870, provided the framework for a system of national education in England.

✓   ✓   ✓

There shall be provided for every school district a sufficient amount of accommodation in public elementary schools (as hereinafter defined) available for all the children resident in such district for whose elementary education efficient and suitable provision is not otherwise made, and where there is an insufficient amount of such accommodation, in this act referred to as "public school accommodations," the deficiency shall be supplied in manner provided by this act.

Where the education department, in the manner provided by this act, are satisfied and have given public notice that there is an insufficient amount of such accommodation for any school district, and the deficiency is not supplied as hereinafter provided, a school board shall be formed for such district and shall supply such deficiency, and in case of default by the school board the education department shall cause the duty of such board to be performed in manner provided by this act. . . .

Every public elementary school shall be conducted in accordance with the following regulations . . . : (1) It shall not be required . . . that he shall attend or abstain from attending . . . any religious observance or any instruction in religious subjects . . . ; (2) The time or times during which religious observance is practised or instruction in religious subjects is given at any meeting of the school shall be either at the beginning or at the end . . . of such meeting . . . ; (3) The school shall be open . . . to the inspection of any of her majesty's inspectors . . . ; (4) The school shall be conducted in accordance with the conditions required to be fulfilled by an elementary school in order to obtain an annual parliamentary grant. . . .

Every school provided by a school board shall be conducted under the control and management of such board in accordance with the following regulations: (1) The school shall be a public elementary school within the meaning of this act; (2) No religious catechism or religious formulary which is distinctive of any particular denomination shall be taught in the school. . . .

Every child attending a school provided by any school board shall pay such weekly fee as may be prescribed by the school board, with the consent of the education department, but the school board may from time to time, for a renewal period not exceeding six months, remit the whole or any part of such fee in the case of any child when they are of opinion that the parent of such child is unable from poverty to pay the same, but such remission shall not be deemed parochial relief given to such parent. . . .

The school board shall be elected in manner provided by this act—in a borough by the persons whose names are on the burgess roll of such borough for the time being in force, and in a parish not situate in the metropolis by the ratepayers. . . .

The school board shall be a body corporate, by the name of the school board of the district to which they belong, having a perpetual succession and a common seal, with power to acquire and hold land. . . .

The school board, not less than one month before submitting any by-law . . . for the approval of the education department, shall deposit a printed copy of the proposed by-laws at their office for inspection by any ratepayer, and shall publish a notice of such deposit. The education department, before approving of any by-laws, shall be satisfied that such deposit has been made and notice published, and shall cause such inquiry to be made in the school district as they think requisite. Any proceeding to enforce any by-law may be taken and any penalty for the breach of any by-law may be recovered in a summary manner; but no penalty imposed for the breach of any by-law shall exceed such amount as with the costs will amount to 5s. for each offence; and such by-laws shall not come into operation until they have been sanctioned by her majesty in council.

THE EMS DISPATCH, JULY 13, 1870

The confused diplomatic meddling of Louis Napoleon, an imperfect carbon-copy version of his uncle, Napoleon Bonaparte, gave Bismarck the chance to strike a final blow for German unity. Anxious to preserve the Napoleonic legend of military invincibility, the French emperor tried to hinder the development of German unification. It was an uneven match. Bismarck isolated Napoleon, making certain that Italy, Russia, Austria, and England would not come to the aid of France. With the Prussian army in a high state of efficiency under General von Moltke, Bismarck awaited his opportunity. The idea was to force the French ruler into a trap from which he would declare war on Prussia.

The conflict came to a head over the projected Hohenzollern candidacy for the throne of Spain. When King William of Prussia was taking the cure at Bad Ems in the middle of July, 1870, he was approached by Benedetti, the French ambassador, and was requested to abandon, once and for all time, any claims to the throne of Spain. Privy Councillor Heinrich Abeken, the writer of official dispatches, telegraphed an account of the meeting to Bismarck, who received it while at dinner in Berlin with Generals von Moltke and von Roon. The hard-bitten militarists had no desire for food after Bismarck read to them the telegram in its original form.

Bismarck edited the dispatch in such a way that the generals immediately recovered their appetites. The telegram was released to the press the next day, July 14, 1870, which happened to be Bastille Day. In its abbreviated form, the telegram gave the impression of an ultimatum. Both the French and German people interpreted it as an unmitigated insult. France declared war immediately.

The Ems Dispatch resulted in an endless controversy among historians. German historians, almost without ex-

133

*ception, insist that it was issued under normal press pro-
cedures, and that, besides, Bismarck was justified in using
any shrewd move in the battle of wits. Non-German historians claim that Bismarck's version of the telegram was
an unscrupulous trick. Bismarck himself was inordinately
proud of his handiwork. The first selection below is his
own version of the incident from his memoirs. The second
gives the original Abeken text and Bismarck's edited version.*

✓   ✓   ✓

A

Bismarck on the Ems Dispatch [62]

I invited Generals Moltke and Roon to have dinner with
me on July 13th, and spoke to them concerning my views
and intentions. During the dinner conversation it was reported to me that a code telegram had been received from
Ems, and it was then in process of decoding. I then read
it to my guests, who were so crushed that they refused to
eat or drink.

All considerations, conscious or unconscious, strengthened my opinion that war could be avoided only at the
cost of the honor of Prussia and of the national confidence
in her.

Under this conviction I made use of the royal authority
communicated to me through Abeken to publish the contents of the telegram. In the presence of my guests I reduced the telegram by deleting words, but without adding
or altering a single word. . . .

The difference in the effect of the shortened text of the
Ems telegram as compared with that of the original was
not the result of stronger words, but of the form, which
made the announcement appear decisive.

After I had read the condensed version to my two
guests, Moltke said:

"Now it has a quite different ring. In its original form
it sounded like a parley. Now it is like a flourish in answer
to a challenge!"

[62] Otto von Bismarck, *Gedanken und Erinnerungen* (J. G.
Cotta'sche Buchhandlung, Stuttgart and Berlin, 1898), II,
406-08.

I went on to explain:

"If, in execution of His Majesty's order, I immediately communicate this text, which contains no changes in or additions to the telegram, not only to the newspapers, but also by wire to all our embassies, it will be known in Paris before midnight. Not only on account of its contents, but also because of the manner of its distribution, it will have the effect of a red flag on the Gallic bull.

"We must fight if we do not want to act the part of the defeated without a battle. However, success depends essentially upon the impression which the beginning of the war makes upon us and others. It is most important that we should be the ones attacked. Gallic insolence and sensitivity will bring this about if we announce before all Europe, as far as we can without the speaking tube of the Reichstag, that we are courageously meeting the public threats of France."

This explanation drew from both generals a metamorphosis into a more joyous mood, whose liveliness surprised me. They had suddenly recovered their desire to eat and drink and began to speak in a more cheerful tone.

Roon said: "Our God of old still lives, and will not let us die in disgrace."

Moltke relinquished his passive equanimity so much that, glancing up joyously to the ceiling and abandoning his usual punctiliousness of speech, he pounded his chest with his hand and exclaimed:

"If I may but live to lead our armies in such a war, then right afterwards let the devil come and haul away the old carcass." He was then more frail than later and had his doubts as to whether he could live through the fatigue of a field campaign.

B

Original and Revised Versions
of the Ems Dispatch [63]

The Abeken Text	Bismarck's Edited Version
Ems, July 13, 1870.	After the news of the re-

[63] Translated by the editor.

To the Federal Chancellor, Count Bismarck, No. 27, No. 61 eod. 3:10 P.M. Station Ems (Rush!)

His Majesty the King writes:

"M. Benedetti accosted me on the promenade, in order to demand of me—most importunately, at last, that I should authorize him to telegraph immediately to Paris that His Majesty the King bound himself for all future time never again to give his consent if the Hohenzollerns renew that candidature. I re-severely, for one may not and cannot make such commitments for ever and ever [à tout jamais]. Naturally, I informed him that I had received no news as yet, and, since he had been informed earlier than I by way of Paris and Madrid, he could easily understand that my Government had no hand in the matter."

Since then His Majesty has received a dispatch from the Prince [Charles Anthony]. As His Majesty has informed Count Benedetti that he was expecting news from the Prince, His Majesty, because of the above-mentioned demand, decided, in consonance with the advice of Count Eulen-

nunciation of the hereditary Prince of Hohenzollern had been officially communicated to the imperial government of France by the royal government of Spain, the French Ambassador at Ems made an additional demand of His Majesty,

that he should authorize him to telegraph to Paris that His Majesty the King bound himself for all future time never again to give his consent if the Hohenzollerns renew that candidature.

berg and mine, not to receive the French envoy again, and informed him through an aide-de-camp on duty that His Majesty had received from the Prince confirmation of the news which Benedetti had already received from Paris, and had nothing further to say to the Ambassador. His Majesty leaves it to Your Ex-lency to determine whether or not this new demand of Benedetti's and its rejection should not be communicated without delay to our representatives and to the press.

His Majesty the King thereupon decided not to receive the French envoy again, and informed him through an aide-de-camp on duty that His Majesty had nothing further to say to the Ambassador.

— 36 —

THE DOGMA OF PAPAL INFALLIBILITY, JULY 18, 1870[64]

At the Vatican Council of 1869-70, the first such council since that of Trent three centuries previously, the traditional teaching of the Church on the relationship between faith and reason was reaffirmed. In a sensational pronouncement, the Council proclaimed the infallibility of the

[64] W. E. Gladstone, *The Vatican Decrees* (New York, and London, 1875), pp. 163-68. The English translation from Archbishop Manning, *Petri Privilegium* (London, 1871), Part III.

Pope and the universality of his episcopate. It was announced as "a dogma divinely revealed" that, when the Pope speaks ex cathedra, *that is, when in discharge of the office of pastor and doctor of all Christians, on any matter of faith and morals, he is possessed of infallibility.*

Catholics insisted that papal infallibility referred only to matters of dogma, faith, and morals. Protestants attacked the concept on the grounds that there is no established or accepted definition of the phrase ex cathedra, *and that all departments and functions of human life fall within the domain of morals. A violent storm raged over the doctrine, with Catholics defending it as merely an ecclesiastical dogma, while Protestants condemned it as a scheme to elevate the papacy above secular governments and to enable it to interfere in national politics. Papal infallibility was denounced by Bismarck and Gladstone, by anti-clericals in France, by revolutionists in Spain, and by liberals in Italy and Austria. Pius IX defended it zealously as the consistent tradition of Catholic Christianity.*

✓   ✓   ✓

Dogmatic Constitution on the Catholic Faith
Published in the Third Session, held April 24, 1870
Pius, Bishop, Servant of the Servants of God,
with the Approval of the Sacred Council,
for Perpetual Remembrance

Chapter IV

Concerning the Infallible Teaching of the
Roman Pontiff

Moreover, that the supreme power of teaching is also included in the Apostolic primacy, which the Roman Pontiff, as the successor of Peter, Prince of the Apostles, possesses over the Whole Church, this Holy See has always held, the perpetual practice of the Church confirms, and oecumenical Councils also have declared, especially those in which the East with the West met in the union of faith and charity. For the Fathers of the Fourth Council of Constantinople, following in the footsteps of their predecessors, gave forth this solemn profession: The first condition of salvation is to keep the rule of the true faith.

And because the sentence of our Lord Jesus Christ can
not be passed by, who said: "Thou art Peter, and upon
this rock I will build my Church" (*Matt.* xvi., 18), these
things which have been said are approved by events, because in the Apostolic See the Catholic religion and her
holy and well-known doctrine has always been kept unde-
filed. Desiring, therefore, not to be in the least degree separated from the faith and doctrine of that See, we hope
that we may deserve to be in one communion, which the
Apostolic See preaches, in which is the entire and true
solidity of the Christian religion. And, with the approval
of the Second Council of Lyons, the Greeks professed that
the holy Roman Church enjoys supreme and full primacy
and preëminence over the whole Catholic Church, which
it truly and humbly acknowledges that it has received
with the plenitude of power from our Lord himself in the
person of blessed Peter, Prince or Head of the Apostles,
whose successor the Roman Pontiff is; and as the Apostolic See is bound before all others to defend the truth of
faith, so also, if any questions arise, they must be defined
by its judgment. Finally, the Council of Florence defined:
That the Roman Pontiff is the true vicar of Christ, and
the head of the whole Church, and the father and teacher
of all Christians; and that to him in blessed Peter was
delivered by our Lord Jesus Christ the full power of feed-
ing, ruling, and governing the whole Church.

To satisfy this pastoral duty, our predecessors have
made unwearied efforts that the salutary doctrine of
Christ might be propagated among all the nations of the
earth, and with equal care watched that it might be preserved genuine and pure where it had been received.
Therefore the Bishops of the whole world, now singly,
now assembled in Synod, following the long-established
custom of churches, and the form of the ancient rule, sent
word to this Apostolic See of those dangers especially
which sprang up in matters of faith, that there the losses
of faith might be most effectually repaired where the faith
cannot fail. And the Roman Pontiffs, according to the
exigencies of times and circumstances, sometimes assembling oecumenical Councils, or asking for the mind of the
Church scatters throughout the world, sometimes by Particular Synods, sometimes using other helps which Di-

vine Providence supplied, defined as to be held those things which with the help of God they had recognized as conformable with the sacred Scriptures and Apostolic traditions. For the Holy Spirit was not promised to the successors of Peter, that by his revelation they might make known new doctrine; but that by his assistance they might inviolably keep and faithfully expound the revelation or deposit of faith delivered through the apostles. And, indeed, all the venerable fathers have embraced, and the holy orthodox doctors have venerated and followed, their Apostolic doctrine; knowing most fully that this See of holy Peter remains ever free from all blemish of error according to the divine promise of the Lord our Saviour made to the Prince of his disciples: "I have prayed for thee that thy faith fail not, and, when thou art converted, confirm thy brethren" (*Luke,* xxii., 32). . . .

Therefore faithfully adhering to the tradition received from the beginning of the Christian faith, for the glory of God our Saviour, the exaltation of the Catholic religion, and the salvation of Christian people, the sacred Council approving, we teach and define that it is a dogma divinely revealed: that the Roman Pontiff, when he speaks *ex cathedra,* that is, when in discharge of the office of pastor and doctor of all Christians, by virtue of his supreme Apostolic authority, he defines a doctrine regarding faith or morals to be held by the universal Church, by the divine assistance promised to him in blessed Peter, is possessed of that infallibility with which the divine Redeemer willed that his Church should be endowed for defining doctrine regarding faith or morals; and that therefore such definitions of the Roman Pontiff are irreformable of themselves, and not from consent of the Church.

But if anyone—which may God avert—presume to contradict this our definition: let him be anathema.

Given at Rome in public Session solemnly held in the Vatican Basilica in the year of our Lord one thousand eight hundred and seventy, on the eighteenth day of July, in the twenty-fifth year of our Pontificate.

37

THE CONSTITUTION OF THE GERMAN EMPIRE, APRIL 16, 1871 [65]

The Constitution of the German Empire, adopted in 1871, was designed to unify the country without affecting the power of the reigning princes. The federal union consisted of twenty-five states enjoying a large measure of local sovereignty. Bavaria retained her own postal and telegraph system; Bavaria, Baden, and Württemberg were relieved of federal taxes on brandy and beer; but civil and criminal law were run by Imperial legislation.

The head of the state, the German Emperor, was also King of Prussia. The upper legislative house, the Bundesrat, was composed of sixty-one members, distributed among the states according to size. The lower body, the Reichstag, was elected by universal manhood suffrage. With no cabinet system, the Chancellor, who was generally at the same time Prussian Prime Minister, directed the policies of the Empire without ministerial responsibility.

The main characteristic of the federal system was the domination of Prussia over the other states of the union. Using her seventeen votes in the Bundesrat as a unit (only fourteen votes were needed to prevent any changes in the Imperial constitution), Prussia controlled the entire political system. The King of Prussia was German Emperor; her Prime Minister was Chancellor; her consent was necessary for any proposed changes in the army, navy, or taxes. In effect, the constitution provided for a semi-autocratic state ruled by the King of Prussia, the Chancellor, and Prussian Junkers and officials. This system was utilized in the belief that it was best adapted for German needs and made for efficiency in government.

[65] Translated from the official German version, 22nd ed. (Leipzig, 1929), *passim*.

PREAMBLE

His Majesty the King of Prussia in the name of the North German Confederation, His Majesty the King of Bavaria, His Majesty the King of Württemberg, His Royal Highness the Grand Duke of Baden, and His Royal Highness the Grand Duke of Hesse and Rhenish Hesse for the areas of the Grand Duchy of Hesse lying north of the Main, hereby establish a perpetual Federation for the protection of the Federation's territory and of the law in effect within that territory, as well as for the maintenance of the welfare of the German People. This Federation shall bear the name German Empire, and shall have the following

CONSTITUTION

1. Federal Territory

ARTICLE 1. The Federal territory consists of the States of Prussia (with Lauenberg), Bavaria, Saxony, Württemberg, Baden, Hesse, Mecklenburg-Schwerin, Saxe-Weimar, Mecklenburg-Strelitz, Oldenburg, Brunswick, Saxe-Meinigen, Saxe-Altenberg, Saxe-Coburg-Gotha, Anhalt, Schwarzburg-Rudolstadt, Schwarzburg-Sondershausen, Waldeck, Reuss of the Elder Line, Reuss of the Younger Line, Schaumburg-Lippe, Lippe, Lübeck, Bremen, and Hamburg.

2. Imperial Legislation

ARTICLE 2. The Empire exercises the right of legislation within the Federal territory according to the provisions of this Constitution, and with the effect that Imperial legislation shall take precedence over State legislation. Imperial legislation holds its binding force through proclamation by the Reich in its Imperial Legislative journal [*Reichsgesetzblatt*]. In so far as no other date is given in this publication for the beginning of the binding force for legislation, it shall come into effect fourteen days following publication.

ARTICLE 3. There shall be a common right of citizenship for all Germany, with the effect that every person (subject, citizen) residing in any federated State shall be treated as a member of any other federated State, and shall be treated equally in such matters as fixed residence, pursuit of a livelihood, eligibility for public office, acquiring of property, achievement of State citizenship, and enjoyment of all special rights of citizenship. . . .

ARTICLE 5. The Imperial legislative power shall be exercised by the *Bundesrat* and the *Reichstag*. The agreement of the majority votes of both bodies is necessary and sufficient for an imperial statute.

3. Bundesrat

ARTICLE 6. The *Bundesrat* is composed of the representatives of the members of the Federation, and the voting procedure shall be as follows: Prussia, together with the former votes of Hanover, Kurhesse, Holstein, Nassau, and Frankfurt, 17 votes; Bavaria, 6; Saxony, 4; Württemberg, 4; Baden, 3; Hesse, 3; Mecklenburg-Schwerin, 2; Brunswick, 2; Saxe-Weimar, 1; Mecklenburg-Strelitz, 1; Oldenburg, 1; Saxe-Meiningen, 1; Saxe-Altenburg, 1; Saxe-Coburg-Gotha, 1; Anhalt, 1; Schwarzburg-Rudelstadt, 1; Schwarzburg-Sondershausen, 1; Waldeck, 1; Reuss of the Elder Line, 1; Reuss of the Younger Line, 1; Schaumburg-Lippe, 1; Lippe, 1; Lübeck, 1; Bremen, 1; Hamburg, 1. Total, 58 votes.

Every member of the Federation can name as many delegates to the *Bundesrat* as it has votes, but all delegations must cast their votes as a unit.

ARTICLE 7. The *Bundesrat* shall decide upon:

1. Proposals made by the *Reichstag* and decisions made by it;

2. The implementation of the general administrative measures and orders necessitated by Imperial legislation, in so far as Imperial legislation has not determined otherwise;

3. The correction of deficiencies that arise in the implementation of Imperial legislation or the abovementioned regulations. . . .

ARTICLE 8. The *Bundesrat* shall organize from its membership permanent committees for (1) the Army and its citadels; (2) the Navy; (3) customs and taxes; (4) trade and communication; (5) railroads, post, and telegraph; (6) judiciary; and (7) accounts.

In each of these committees, outside of the chairman, four Federal States must be represented, and each State shall have but one vote. . . .

ARTICLE 9. Every member of the *Bundesrat* has the right to appear in the Reichstag, and, on demand, must be heard each time, in order to represent the views of his Government, even if these views have not been adopted by the majority of the *Bundesrat*. No one can simultaneously be a member of the *Bundesrat* and the *Reichstag*.

ARTICLE 10. The Emperor shall have the duty of providing ordinary diplomatic protection for the members of the *Bundesrat*.

4. Presiding Officer

ARTICLE 11. The Presiding Officer of the Federation shall be the King of Prussia, who shall bear the name *German Emperor*. The Emperor shall represent the Empire in the Law of Nations, to declare war and conclude peace in the name of the Empire, to enter into alliances and other treaties with foreign States, to accredit and receive ambassadors.

The consent of the *Bundesrat* is required for a declaration of war in the name of the Empire, with the exception of cases of an attack upon the territory of the Empire or its coasts.

ARTICLE 12. The Emperor summons, opens, prorogues, and closes the *Bundesrat* and the *Reichstag*.

ARTICLE 13. The *Bundesrat* and the *Reichstag* shall be summoned annually. For the preparation of these meetings, the *Bundesrat* can be summoned without the *Reichstag,* but the latter cannot be summoned without the *Bundesrat*.

ARTICLE 14. The *Bundesrat* must be summoned immediately after such a demand by one-third of its membership.

ARTICLE 15. The presiding chair in the *Bundesrat* and the conduct of business appertain to the Imperial Chancellor who is to be appointed by the Emperor. . . .

5. Reichstag

ARTICLE 20. The *Reichstag* shall proceed from universal and direct elections with secret voting. . . .

ARTICLE 21. Public officials are not permitted vacations in order to serve in the *Reichstag*. . . .

ARTICLE 22. The meetings of the *Reichstag* shall be public. . . .

ARTICLE 23. The *Reichstag* shall have the right, within the competence of Imperial legislation, to present and to pass on petitions directed to it to the *Bundesrat* and the Imperial Chancellor.

ARTICLE 24. The legislative period of the *Reichstag* lasts five years. For the dissolution of the Reichstag during this period a resolution of the *Bundesrat* with the concurrence of the Emperor is required. . . .

ARTICLE 28. The *Reichstag* acts with an absolute majority. The presence of a majority of the legal number of members is required for the validity of its action. . . .

ARTICLE 76. Controversies between different members of the Federation, in so far as they are not of a private-law nature and therefore to be decided by the competent tribunals, shall be disposed of by the *Bundesrat* upon application of one of the parties. . . .

ARTICLE 78. Amendments of the Constitution are made by way of legislation. They shall be considered as rejected if they have fourteen votes against them in the *Bundesrat*.

Those provisions of the Imperial Constitution, by which certain rights of individual members of the Federation in their relations to the whole are determined, can be amended only with the consent of the member of the Federation entitled to said rights.

38

THE END OF THE FRANCO-PRUSSIAN WAR, MAY 10, 1871

Bismarck succeeded in founding the Second Reich even before peace was concluded. While the siege of Paris was approaching its final stage, the long struggle for national unity ended in a memorable ceremony. On January 18, 1871, one hundred and seventy years after the coronation of Frederick I as the first Prussian king (King in Prussia), *William I was proclaimed German Emperor in the Hall of Mirrors of the Palace of Versailles. With this proud military ceremony the Second Reich was born and Germany took a place on the world scene as a great power.*

The final peace negotiations with France were signed at Frankfurt am Main on May 10, 1871. The new western boundary of Germany was to include Alsace and Lorraine, over which France and Germany had fought for a thousand years, and which were now combined as a province (Reichsland) *of the new Reich. German security now seemed assured by possession of the fortresses of Metz and Strassburg. The war indemnity was fixed at five billion gold francs, an enormous sum at that time. Even if Bismarck had desired it, an easy peace such as that concluded in 1866 after the Austro-Prussian war would have been impossible, considering the demands of the army and public opinion. The Peace of Frankfurt made it certain that, one day, France would seek* revanche.

✦   ✦   ✦

A

The Imperial Proclamation, January 18, 1871 [66]

[66] Horst Kohl, ed., *Die politische Reden des Fürsten von Bismarck; historische-kritische Gesammtausgabe* (14 vols.; Stuttgart, 1882-1904), IV, 444.

Whereas, the German Princes and the Free Cities have called unanimously upon us to revive and assume, with the restoration of the German Empire, the German imperial office, which has not been occupied for more than sixty years, and

Whereas, adequate arrangements have been made for this purpose in the Constitution of the German Confederation;

Therefore, we, William, by the grace of God, King of Prussia, do hereby proclaim that we have considered it to be a duty to our common Fatherland to respond to the summons of the unified German Princes and cities and to accept the German imperial title. As a result, we and those who succeed us on the throne of Prussia, henceforth, shall bear the imperial title in all our relations and in all the activities of the German Empire, and we trust to God that the German nation will be granted the ability to construct a propitious future for the Fatherland under the symbol of its ancient glory.

We assume the imperial title, aware of the duty of protecting, with German loyalty, the rights of the Empire and of its members, of maintaining the peace, and of protecting the independent rulers of Germany, which, in turn, is dependent upon the united power of the people.

We assume the title in the hope that the German people will be granted the ability to enjoy the fruits of its zealous and self-sacrificing wars in eternal peace, inside boundaries that give the Fatherland a security against renewed French aggression which has been lost for centuries. May God grant that we and our successors on the imperial throne may at all times enhance the wealth of the German Empire, not through military conquests, but by the blessings and the gifts of peace, within the realm of national prosperity, freedom, and morality.

Issued at General Headquarters, Versailles, January 18, 1871.

WILLIAM

B

Excerpts from the Peace of Frankfurt, May 10, 1871 [67]

ARTICLE 1. The distance from the city of Belfort to the frontier line, such as it was first proposed at the time of the negotiations at Versailles, and such as is marked on the map annexed to the instrument ratified by the preliminary treaty of the 26th of February, is considered as indicating the measure of the radius which, in virtue of the clause relative to it from the first article of the preliminaries, is to remain with France together with the city and fortifications of Belfort.

The international commission with which Article 1 of the preliminaries is concerned shall remain on the territory immediately after the exchange of ratifications of the present treaty in order to execute the tasks which devolves upon it and in order to make the draft of the new frontier conform to the preceding dispositions. . . .

ARTICLE 3. The French Government shall return to the German Government the archives, documents, and registries concerning the civil, military, and judicial administration of the ceded territories. If any one of these titles have been displaced, they shall be restored by the French Government on the demand of the German Government. . . .

ARTICLE 5. The two nations shall possess equal rights in navigation on the Moselle, the Rhine Canal to the Marne, the Rhône Canal to the Rhine, the Saar Canal, and the navigable waters communicating with routes of navigation. The right of flotage shall be maintained. . . .

ARTICLE 7. The payment of five hundred millions [francs] shall take place in the thirty days which follow the re-establishment of the authority of the French Government in the city of Paris. One billion shall be paid during the course of the year, and a half billion by the 1st of

[67] *Der deutsch-französische Krieg.* The War Historical Division of the Great General Staff (Berlin, 1872-81), part 2, section 20, pp. 799 ff. Translated from the French.

May, 1872. The three final billions shall be payable on the 2nd of March, 1874, as has been stipulated by the preliminary peace treaty. After the 2nd of March of the current year, the interest on these three billions of francs shall be paid each year, on the 3rd of March, at the rate of 5% per year. . . . After the payment of the first half-billion and the ratification of the definite treaty of peace, the Departments of the Somme, the Lower Seine, and the Eure shall be evacuated in so far as they are still occupied by German troops. The evacuation of the Departments of the Oise, Seine-et-Oise, Seine-et-Marne, and the Seine, as well as the forts of Paris, shall take place as soon as the German Government shall decide that sufficient order has been established in France as well as in Paris in order to assure the execution of the contracted engagements by France.

In all cases, that evacuation shall take place at the time of the payment of the third half-billion.

ARTICLE 8. The German troops will continue to refrain from taking requisitions in kind or in money from the occupied territories; this obligation on their part being correlative to the contractual obligations for their support by the French Government,—in the case where, in spite of the reiterated claims of the German Government, the French Government should be late in executing the said obligations, the German troops shall have the right to procure that which is necessary for their needs in raising the imposts and the requisitions in the occupied Departments and even outside of them, if their resources are not sufficient. . . .

ARTICLE 10. The German Government, in understanding with the French Government, shall continue to return prisoners of war. The French Government, on their part, shall return those of the prisoners who are ready to be exchanged. As for those who have not finished their term of service, they shall retire behind the Loire. It is understood that the army of Paris and Versailles, after the establishment of the authority of the French Government in Paris and until the evacuation of the forts by German troops, shall not exceed 24,000 men. . . .

ARTICLE 12. All expelled Germans shall keep full

and entire possession of all the property they have acquired in France. . . .

ARTICLE 16. The two Governments, German and
French, bind themselves reciprocally to respect and preserve the graves of the buried soldiers on their respective
territories. . . .

ARTICLE 18. The ratifications of the present treaty
by His Majesty, the Emperor of Germany,* on the one
side, and by the National Assembly and the Executive
Chief of Power of the French Republic, on the other,
shall be exchanged at Frankfurt within ten days or
sooner, if possible.

Issued at Frankfurt, May 10, 1871.

(Signed) V. BISMARCK
         ARNIM
             (Signed) JULES FAVRE
                      POUYER-QUERTIER
                      E. DE GOULARD

— 39 —

LAWS ON THE EXECUTIVE POWER IN FRANCE, 1871-73

*The laws on the executive authority in France from
1871 to 1873 reflected the violent struggle for control
between republicans and royalists. The Rivet Law of
August 31, 1871 provided for a President of the Third
French Republic, but, in view of Louis Napoleon's coup*

* In the French text, *l'Empereur d'Allemagne* is the term used.
The title was *German Emperor*, not *Emperor of Germany*.

d'état *in 1851, the document carefully made the President responsible to the Assembly. The royalists continued to denounce the Republic as "a breeder of radicalism, anarchy, and moral chaos." In 1873 the Assembly forced the resignation of Thiers, and chose as his successor, Marshal MacMahon, a zealous royalist. The Law of the Septennate, November 20, 1873, specifically naming Marshal MacMahon as President, extended his term to seven years, as a step towards restoration of the monarchy.*

✓   ✓   ✓

A

The Rivet Law, August 31, 1871 [68]

THE NATIONAL ASSEMBLY . . . decrees:

1. The head of the executive power shall take the title of President of the French Republic and shall continue to exercise, under the authority of the National Assembly, so long as it shall not have terminated its labors, the functions that were delegated to him by the decree of February 17, 1871.

2. The President of the Republic promulgates the laws as soon as they are transmitted to him by the president of the National Assembly.

He secures and supervises the exercise of the laws.

He resides at the place where the National Assembly sits.

He is heard by the National Assembly whenever he believes it necessary and after he has informed the president of the National Assembly of his desires.

He appoints and dismisses the ministers. The Council of Ministers and the ministers are responsible to the Assembly.

Each of the acts of the President of the Republic must be countersigned by a minister.

3. The President of the Republic is responsible to the Assembly.

[68] J. B. Duvergier, ed., *et al., Collection complète des lois, décrets, ordonnances, règlements, avis du Conseil d'État,* 2nd ed., 31 vols. (Paris. 1834-   ), LXXI, 210-12.

B

Law of the Septennate, November 20, 1873 [69]

1. The executive power is entrusted for seven years to Marshal de MacMahon, Duke of Magenta, dating from the promulgation of the present law.

This power shall continue to be exercised with the title of President of the Republic and under the existing conditions until the modifications which may be expected therein by the constitutional laws.

2. Within the three days which follow the promulgation of the present law, a commission of 30 members shall be selected in public and by *scrutin de liste,* for the consideration of the constitutional laws.

— 40 —

STANLEY FINDS LIVINGSTONE, NOVEMBER 10, 1871 [70]

European interest in Africa in the early nineteenth century was stimulated by the stories of missionaries, traders, and adventurers. It was not until the second half of the century, however, that the great continent came to be regarded as an area suitable for the new imperialism. In March, 1866, David Livingstone (1813-1873), a Scottish explorer-missionary, landed on the shore of East Africa, and shortly thereafter disappeared in the bush. From that time until his death only one Westerner was to see him again. Livingstone's explorations had a double purpose—to find the source of the Nile

[69] *Ibid.,* LXXIII, 363-68.
[70] *The New York Herald,* August 10, 1872.

and to bring the slave trade to an end. To resolve all doubts concerning Livingstone's fate and to build up newspaper circulation, James Gordon Bennett, Jr., the enterprising proprietor of The New York Herald, *commissioned one of his star reporters, Henry Morton Stanley, (1841-1894) to equip an expedition to search for the lost explorer. The meeting of reporter and explorer on November 10, 1871 made one of the most famous newspaper stories of the nineteenth century.*

Livingstone's explorations in the regions of the Congo River, Lake Tanganyika, and Northern Rhodesia, and Stanley's stories of pigmies, Amazons, cannibals, exotic animals, rubber-producing plants, and other wonders of the Dark Continent precipitated an undignified scramble for Africa among the great powers. Fired with ambition, hundreds of explorers hit the African trail.

The following extracts are from Stanley's great journalistic scoop.

BUNDER IJIBI,[71] ON LAKE TANGANYIKA, CENTRAL AFRICA, NOVEMBER 23, 1871—Only two months gone, and what a change in my feelings! But two months ago, what a peevish, fretful soul was mine! What a hopeless prospect presented itself before your correspondent! Arabs vowing that I would never behold Tanganyika; Sheik, the son of Nahib, declaring me a madman to his fellows because I would not heed his words. My own men deserting, my servants whining day by day, and my white man endeavoring to impress me with the belief that they were all doomed men! And the only answer to it all is Livingstone, the hero traveler, is alongside of me, writing as hard as he can to his friends in England, India, and America, and I am quite safe and sound in health and limb. Wonderful, is it not, that such a thing should be, when the seers had foretold that it would be otherwise—that all my schemes, that all my determination, would avail me nothing? But probably you are in as much of a hurry to know how it all took place as I am to relate. So, to the recital.

[71] Anglo-Indian for harbor.

September 23 I left Unyanyembe, driving before me fifty well-armed black men, loaded with the goods of the expedition, and dragging after me one white man. Several Arabs stood by my late residence to see the last of me and mine, as they felt assured that there was not the least hope of their ever seeing me again. Shaw, the white man, was as pale as death, and would willingly have received the order to stop behind in Unyanyembe, only he had not quite the courage to ask permission, from the fact that only the night before he had expressed a hope that I would not leave him behind, and I had promised to give him a good riding donkey and to walk after him until he recovered perfect health. However, as I gave the order to march, some of the men, in a hurry to obey the order, managed to push by him suddenly and down he went like a dead man. The Arabs, thinking doubtless that I would not go now because my white subordinate seemed so ill, hurried in a body to the fallen man, loudly crying at what they were pleased to term my cruelty and obstinacy; but, pushing them back, I mounted Shaw on his donkey, and told them that I must see Tanganyika first, as I had sworn to go on. . . .

Once away from the hateful valley of Kwihara, once out of sight of the obnoxious fields, my enthusiasm for my work rose as newborn as when I left the coast. But my enthusiasm was short-lived, for before reaching camp I was almost delirious with fever. . . .

Near Isinga met a caravan of eighty Waguha direct from Ujiji, bearing oil, and bound for Unyanyembe. They report that a white man was left by them five days ago at Ujiji. He had the same color as I have, wears the same shoes, the same clothes, and has hair on his face like I have, only his is white. This is Livingstone. Hurrah for Ujiji! My men share my joy, for we shall be coming back now directly; and, being so happy at the prospect, I buy three goats and five gallons of native beer, which will be eaten and drank directly. . . .

We are now about descending—in a few minutes we shall have reached the spot where we imagine the object of our search—our fate will soon be decided. No one in that town knows we are coming; least of all do they

know we are so close to them. If any of them ever heard
of the white man at Unyanyembe they must believe we
are there yet. We shall take them all by surprise, for no
other but a white man would dare leave Unyanyembe
for Ujiji with the country in such a distracted state—
no other but a crazy white man, whom Sheik, the son
of Nasib, is going to report to Syed or Prince Burghash
for not taking his advice.

Well, we are but a mile from Ujiji now, and it is high
time that we let them know that a caravan is coming;
so "Commence firing" is the word passed along the
length of the column, and gladly do they begin. They
have loaded their muskets half full, and they roar like
a broadside of a line-of-battle ship. Down go the ram-
rods, sending huge charges home to the breech, and
volley after volley is fired. The flags are fluttered; the
banner of America is in front, waving joyfully; the
guide is in the zenith of his glory. The former residents
of Zanzita will know it directly and will wonder—as
well they may—as to what it means. Never were the
Stars and Stripes so beautiful in my mind—the breeze
of the Tanganyika has such an effect on them. The
guide blows his horn, and the shrill, wild clangor of it
is far and near; and still the cannon muskets tell the
noisy seconds.

By this time the Arabs are fully alarmed; the natives
of Ujiji, Waguha, Warundi, Wanguana, and I know
not whom hurry up by the hundreds to ask what it all
means—this fusillading, shouting, and blowing of horns
and flag flying. There are Yambos shouted out to me
by the dozen, and delighted Arabs have run up breath-
lessly to shake my hand and ask anxiously where I come
from. But I have no patience with them. The expedition
goes far too slow. I should like to settle the vexed question by one personal view. Where is he? Has he fled?

Suddenly a man—a black man—at my elbow shouts in
English, "How do you do, sir?"

"Hello, who the deuce are you?"

"I am the servant of Dr. Livingstone," he says; and before I can ask any more questions he is running like a
madman towards the town.

We have at last entered the town. There are hundreds

of people around me—I might say thousands without exaggeration, it seems to me. It is a grand triumphal procession. As we move, they move. All eyes are drawn towards us. The expedition at last comes to a halt; the journey is ended for a time; but I alone have a few more steps to make.

There is a group of the most respectful Arabs, and as I come nearer I see the white face of an old man among them. He has a cap with a gold band around it, his dress is a short jacket of red blanket cloth, and his pants—well, I didn't observe. I am shaking hands with him. We raise our hats, and I say:

"Dr. Livingstone, I presume?"

And he says, "Yes."

Finis coronat opus.[72]

— 41 —

THE TREATY OF BERLIN, JULY 13, 1878 [73]

The reconstruction of Europe, undertaken by the Congress of Vienna in 1815, was shaken by the events of 1870, which saw the emergence of Germany and Italy as Great Powers. After the three wars of national unification, Bismarck believed that Germany, for the time being, was satiated, and needed time to digest her conquests. When the peace of Europe was threatened in 1878 by a clash of

[72] The end crowns the work.
[73] E. Hertslet, ed., *The Map of Europe by Treaty* (New York and London, 1875-91), IV, p. 2759 ff.

interests between England and Russia, he became an "honest broker" (ehrlicher Makler) *between the two powers, and, at the same time, began organizing his system of military alliances pledged to the maintenance of the* status quo *as fixed by the events of 1870-71.*

In 1821, the Greeks rebelled against Turkish rule, and, with foreign help, obtained their independence in 1829. When Russia tried to drive to the Mediterranean through the Ottoman Empire, England stopped her in the Crimean War (1853-56). When the Turks, under the leadership of Abdul Hamid II, a creature half fox, half rat, slaughtered the Bulgarians in a series of atrocities, Russia, in 1877, declared war on Turkey. By the Treaty of San Stefano (1878), signed by Russia and Turkey, Turkish rule was virtually obliterated in Europe. England refused to sit by tamely and watch Turkey dismembered to the advantage of Russia. There was no doubt that England would go to war again to prevent Russian penetration through the Dardanelles to the Mediterranean.

In this critical situation a congress of the powers met in Berlin, with Bismarck as its president, Disraeli representing England, and Prince Gortschakov as leading Russian delegate. The Treaty of Berlin took away half of Turkey's European territory, and then solemnly guaranteed the "integrity of Turkey." The Near Eastern Question was by no means solved, as disappointed irredentists immediately demanded revision. For England it was "peace with honor." In Bismarck's opinion, the whole Near Eastern Question was not worth "the bones of a Pomeranian grenadier." Germany was not as yet interested in Turkey.

Attention is directed especially to Article 25, by which Austria-Hungary was given the right to occupy and administer the provinces of Bosnia and Herzegovina, which were to remain legally parts of Turkey. Taking advantage of confusion in the Turkish Empire and Russia's weakness due to the war of 1904-05, Vienna on October 6, 1908 announced the formal annexation of Bosnia and Herzegovina to the Austro-Hungarian Empire. This led to the crisis of 1908, which helped pave the way for World War I.

ARTICLE 1. Bulgaria is constituted an autonomous and tributary Principality under the suzerainty of His Imperial Majesty the Sultan; it will have a Christian Government and a national militia.

[ARTICLE 2 defines the exact boundaries of Bulgaria.]

The Prince of Bulgaria shall be freely elected by the population and confirmed by the Sublime Porte, with the assent of the Powers. No member of the reigning dynasties of the Great European Powers may be elected Prince of Bulgaria. . . .

ARTICLE 4. An Assembly of Notables of Bulgaria, convoked at Tirnovo, shall, before the election of the Prince, draw up the Organic Law of the Principality. In the districts where Bulgarians are intermixed with Turkish, Romanian, Greek or other Populations, the rights and interests of these populations shall be taken into consideration as regards the elections and the drawing up of the Organic Law. . . .

ARTICLE 13. A province is formed south of the Balkans which will take the name of "Eastern Roumelia," and will remain under the direct political and military authority of His Imperial Majesty the Sultan, under conditions of administrative autonomy. It shall have a Christian Governor-General. . . .

ARTICLE 25. The Provinces of Bosnia and Herzegovina shall be occupied and administered by Austria-Hungary. The Government of Austria-Hungary, not desiring to undertake the administration of the Sandjak of Novi-Bazar, which extends between Serbia and Montenegro in a south-easterly direction to the other side of Mitrviotza, the Ottoman Administration will continue to exercise its functions there. Nevertheless, in order to assure the maintenance of the new political state of affairs, as well as freedom and security of communications, Austria-Hungary reserves the right of keeping garrisons and having military and commercial roads in the whole of this part of the ancient Vilayet of Bosnia. . . .

ARTICLE 26. The independence of Montenegro is recognized by the Sublime Porte and by all those of the

High Contracting Parties who had not hitherto admitted
it.

ARTICLE 34. The High Contracting Parties recognize
the independence of the Principality of Serbia. . . .

ARTICLE 43. The High Contracting Parties recognize
the independence of Roumania, subject to . . . [the conditions about the same as with Serbia.]

ARTICLE 52. In order to increase the guarantees
which assure the freedom of navigation on the Danube
which is recognized as of European interest, the High
Contracting Parties determine that all the fortresses and
fortification existing on the course of the river from the
Iron Gates to its mouths shall be razed, and no new ones
erected. No vessel of war shall navigate the Danube below the Iron Gates with the exception of vessels of light
tonage in the service of the river police and Customs. The
"stationnaires" of the Powers at the mouths of the Danube
may, however, ascend the river as far as Galatz.

ARTICLE 53. The European Commission of the Danube on which Roumania shall be represented is maintained
in its functions, and shall exercise them henceforth as far
as Galatz in complete independence of the territorial authorities. . . .

ARTICLE 61. The Sublime Porte undertakes to carry
out, without further delay, the improvements and reforms
demanded by local requirements in the provinces inhabited
by the Armenians, and to guarantee their security against
the Circassians and Kurds.

It will periodically make known the steps taken to this
effect to the Powers, who will superintend their application.

THE DUAL ALLIANCE BETWEEN AUSTRIA-HUNGARY AND GERMANY, OCTOBER 7, 1879[74]

There was an outburst of indignation in Russia after the Congress of Berlin in 1878, for the results of which the Russians held Bismarck responsible. For the time being, it seemed impossible to maintain the coöperative spirit between Russia and Germany inaugurated by the Three Emperors' Conferences of 1872-1873. Bismarck decided to choose between Russia and Austria-Hungary. Although Russia was obviously the stronger, she was not Bismarck's choice when the option had to be made. Bismarck chose Austria for a number of reasons: (1) He reasoned that the choice of the weaker partner would more than counterbalance the stronger, while two strong partners might well come to blows; (2) There was a community of interest and "blood" between Germans and Austrians; (3) Any difficulties with Austria would reopen the wounds of 1866 and throw her into the arms of France; (4) An alliance with Russia would preclude the possibility of an alliance with England; and (5) Austria and Russia might conclude an alliance to the exclusion of Germany.

The Dual Alliance of 1879 was one of the most important diplomatic steps of Bismarck's later career. For the next three decades this alliance was to remain the pivot of the European states system.

[74] Reprinted by permission of the publishers from Alfred F. Pribram, editor, *The Secret Treaties of Austria-Hungary, 1879-1914* (translated by Archibald Cary Coolidge), [Cambridge, Mass.: Harvard University Press, 1920], I, 25-31.

ARTICLE 1. Should, contrary to their hope, and against the loyal desire of the two High Contracting Parties, one of the two Empires be attacked by Russia, the High Contracting Parties are bound to come to the assistance one of the other with the whole war strength of their Empires, and accordingly only to conclude peace together and upon mutual agreement.

ARTICLE 2. Should one of the High Contracting Parties be attacked by another Power, the other High Contracting Party binds itself hereby, not only not to support the aggressor against its high Ally, but to observe at least a benevolent neutral attitude towards its fellow Contracting Party.

Should, however, the attacking party in such a case be supported by Russia, either by an active coöperation or by military measures which constitute a menace to the Party attacked, then the obligation stipulated in Article 1 of this Treaty, for reciprocal assistance with the whole fighting force, becomes equally operative, and the conduct of the war by the two High Contracting Parties shall in this case also be in common until the conclusion of a common peace.

ARTICLE 3. The duration of this Treaty shall be provisionally fixed at five years from the day of ratification. One year before the expiration of this period the two High Contracting Parties shall consult together concerning the question whether the conditions serving as the basis of the Treaty still prevail, and reach an agreement in regard to the further continuance or possible modification of certain details. If in the course of the first month of the last year of the Treaty no invitation has been received from either side to open these negotiations, the Treaty shall be considered as renewed for a further period of three years.

ARTICLE 4. This Treaty shall, in conformity with its peaceful character, and to avoid any misinterpretation, be kept secret by the two High Contracting Parties, and only communicated to a third Power upon a joint understanding between the two Parties, and according to the terms of a special Agreement.

The two High Contracting Parties venture to hope, after the sentiments expressed by the Emperor Alexander at the meeting at Alexandrovo, that the armaments of Russia will not in reality prove to be menacing to them, and have on that account no reason for making a communication at present; should, however, this hope, contrary to their expectations, prove to be erroneous, the two High Contracting Parties would consider it their loyal obligation to let the Emperor Alexander know, at least confidentially, that they must consider an attack on either of them as directed against both.

ARTICLE 5. This Treaty shall derive its validity from the approbation of the two Exalted Sovereigns and shall be ratified within fourteen days after this approbation has been granted by Their Most Exalted Majesties.

In witness whereof the Plenipotentiaries have signed this Treaty with their own hands and affixed their arms.

Done at Vienna, October 7, 1879

(L.S.) ANDRÁSSY   (L.S.) H. VII v. REUSS

— 43 —

THE THREE EMPERORS' LEAGUE, JUNE 18, 1881 [75]

In 1881, Bismarck was able to restore the friendly contacts between Austria and Russia that had been undermined by the Congress of Berlin. He strengthened Germany's relations with both Powers by fashioning the Three Emperors' League (Dreikaiserbund). *Bismarck*

[75] Reprinted by permission of the publishers from Alfred F. Pribram, editor, *The Secret Treaties of Austria-Hungary, 1879-1914* (translated by Archibald Cary Coolidge), [Cambridge, Mass.: Harvard University Press, 1920], I, 37 ff.

was certain that his new alliance would prevent an Austro-Russian war or a Franco-Russian coalition. By this agreement, each of the parties promised to remain neutral if either of the others were at war. It was agreed that there should be no changes in European Turkey without common consent, that Turkey keep the Straits closed to all non-Turkish war vessels, and that Bulgaria and Eastern Rumelia could unite if they wished.

Bismarck regarded this agreement as so secret that he refused to entrust the negotiations to the chancery secretaries and wrote out the documents with his own hand. The Three Emperors' League was renewed in 1884 and terminated in 1887.

The Courts of Austria-Hungary, of Germany, and of Russia, animated by an equal desire to consolidate the general peace by an understanding intended to assure the defensive position of their respective States, have come into agreement on certain questions. . . .

With this purpose the three Courts . . . have agreed on the following Articles:

ARTICLE 1. In case one of the High Contracting Parties should find itself at war with a fourth Great Power, the two others shall maintain towards it a benevolent neutrality and shall devote their efforts to the localization of the conflict.

This stipulation shall apply likewise to a war between one of the three Powers and Turkey, but only in the case where a previous agreement shall have been reached between the three Courts as to the results of this war.

In the special case where one of them shall obtain a more positive support from one of its two Allies, the obligatory value of the present Article shall remain in all its force for the third.

ARTICLE 2. Russia, in agreement with Germany, declares her firm resolution to respect the interests arising from the new position assured to Austria-Hungary by the Treaty of Berlin.

The three Courts, desirous of avoiding all discord between them, engage to take account of their respective interests in the Balkan Peninsula. They further promise one another that any new modifications in the territorial status quo of Turkey in Europe can be accomplished only in virtue of a common agreement between them.

In order to facilitate the agreement contemplated by the present Article, an agreement of which it is impossible to foresee all the conditions, the three Courts from the present moment record in the Protocol annexed to this Treaty the points on which an understanding has already been established in principle.

ARTICLE 3. The three Courts recognize the European and mutually obligatory character of the principle of the closing of the Straits of the Bosporus and of the Dardanelles, founded on international law, confirmed by treaties, and summed up in the declaration of the second Plenipotentiary of Russia at the session of July 12 of the Congress of Berlin.

They will take care in common that Turkey shall make no exception to this rule in favor of the interests of any Government whatsoever, by lending to warlike operations of a belligerent Power the portion of its Empire constituted by the Straits.

In case of infringement, or to prevent it if such infringement should be in prospect, the three Courts will inform Turkey that they would regard her, in that event, as putting herself in a state of war towards the injured Party, and as having deprived herself thenceforth of the benefits of the security assured to her territorial status quo by the Treaty of Berlin.

ARTICLE 4. The present Treaty shall be in force during a period of three years, dating from the day of the exchange of ratifications.

ARTICLE 5. The High Contracting Parties mutually promise secrecy as to the contents and the existence of the present Treaty, as well as of the Protocol annexed thereto.

ARTICLE 6. The secret Conventions concluded between Austria-Hungary and Russia and between Germany and Russia in 1873 are replaced by the present Treaty. . . .

SZÉCHÉNYI
v. BISMARCK
SABOUROFF

SEPARATE PROTOCOL ON THE SAME DATE TO THE
CONVENTION OF BERLIN. JUNE 18, 1881

1. *Bosnia and Herzegovina.* Austria-Hungary reserves
the right to annex these provinces at whatever moment
she shall deem opportune.

2. *Sanjak of Novibazar.* The Declaration exchanged
between the Austro-Hungarian Plenipotentiaries and the
Russian Plenipotentiaries at the Congress of Berlin under
the date of July 13/1, 1878, remains in force.

3. *Eastern Rumelia.* The three Powers agree in regarding the eventuality of an occupation either of Eastern
Rumelia or of the Balkans as full of perils for the general
peace. In case this should occur, they will employ their
efforts to dissuade the Porte from such an enterprise,
it being well understood that Bulgaria and Eastern Rumelia on their part are to abstain from provoking the
Porte by attacks emanating from their territories against
the other provinces of the Ottoman Empire.

4. *Bulgaria.* The three Powers will not oppose the eventual reunion of Bulgaria and Eastern Rumelia within the
territorial limits assigned to them by the Treaty of Berlin, if this question should come up by the force of circumstances. They agree to dissuade the Bulgarians from
all aggression against the neighboring provinces, particularly Macedonia; and to inform them that in such a
case they will be acting at their own risk and peril.

5. In order to avoid collisions of interests in the local
questions which may arise, the three Courts will furnish
their representatives and agents in the Orient with a general instruction, directing them to endeavor to smooth out
their divergences by friendly explanations between themselves in each special case; and, in the cases where they
do not succeed in doing so, to refer the matters to their
Governments.

6. The present Protocol forms an integral part of the
secret Treaty signed on this day at Berlin and shall have
the same force and validity. . . .

44

THE TRIPLE ALLIANCE, MAY 20, 1882 [76]

In 1882, Bismarck further amplified his system of treaties by drawing Germany, Austria-Hungary, and Italy into a Triple Alliance. The initiative by which the Dual Alliance became the Triple Alliance came from Italy. After 1871, Bismarck had encouraged France in her colonial ambitions, seeking by this means to distract her from thoughts of revanche. In 1881, France seized Tunisia, which contained a hundred Italians to one Frenchman. Without support, Italy was in no position to challenge French claims. She was defeated in her attempt to conquer Abyssinia and now she looked to Tripoli. To achieve her ambitions in northern Africa and the Adriatic, Italy determined to have a powerful ally at her back. Moreover, she desired assistance in the event of a possible attempt by France to restore the temporal power of the Pope.

Bismarck was not at all averse, under the circumstances, to the overtures of Crispi. A solid block of Central European powers would make France consider carefully before she engaged in a war of revenge. Austria's motive was to achieve security against an attack by Russia; for this security she was willing to come to terms even with the Italians. Driven out of both Germany and Italy, the Austrians might well find compensation by expansion in the Balkans.

Bismarck was now close to his aim of keeping France, potentially his strongest enemy, in isolation. It was an

[76] Reprinted by permission of the publishers from Alfred F. Pribram, editor, *The Secret Treaties of Austria-Hungary, 1879-1914* (translated by Archibald Cary Coolidge), [Cambridge, Mass.: Harvard University Press, 1920], I, 65, 67, 69.

amazing display of diplomatic ingenuity as the German Chancellor succeeded in "keeping five balls in the air at once."

ARTICLE 1. The High Contracting Parties mutually promise peace and friendship, and will enter into no alliance or engagement directed against any one of their States.

They engage to proceed to an exchange of ideas on political and economic questions of a general nature which may arise, and they further promise one another mutual support within the limits of their own interests.

ARTICLE 2. In case Italy, without direct provocation on her part, should be attacked by France for any reason whatsoever, the two other Contracting Parties shall be be bound to lend help and assistance with all their forces to the Party attacked.

This same obligation shall devolve upon Italy in case of any aggression without direct provocation by France against Germany.

ARTICLE 3. If one, or two, of the High Contracting Parties, without direct provocation on their part, should chance to be attacked and to be engaged in a war with two or more Great Powers nonsignatory to the present Treaty, the *casus foederis* will arise simultaneously for all the High Contracting Parties.

ARTICLE 4. In case a Great Power nonsignatory to the present Treaty should threaten the security of the states of one of the High Contracting Parties, and the threatened Party should find itself forced on that account to make war against it, the two others bind themselves to observe towards their Ally a benevolent neutrality. Each of them reserves to itself, in this case, the right to take part in the war, if it should see fit, to make common cause with its Ally.

ARTICLE 5. If the peace of any of the High Contracting Parties should chance to be threatened under the circumstances foreseen by the preceding Articles, the High Contracting Parties shall take counsel together in ample time as to the military measures to be taken with a view to eventual coöperation.

They engage henceforward, in all cases of common participation in a war, to conclude neither armistice, nor peace, nor treaty, except by common agreement among themselves.

ARTICLE 6. The High Contracting Parties mutually promise secrecy as to the contents and existence of the present Treaty.

ARTICLE 7. The present Treaty shall remain in force during the space of five years, dating from the day of the exchange of ratifications.

ARTICLE 8. The ratifications of the present Treaty shall be exchanged at Vienna within three weeks, or sooner if may be.

In witness whereof the respective Plenipotentiaries have signed the present Treaty and have affixed thereto the seal of their arms.

Done at Vienna, the twentieth day of the month of May of the year one thousand eight hundred and eighty-two.

(L.S.) KÁLNOKY
(L.S.) H. VII OF REUSS
(L.S.) C. ROBILANT

[*An additional Declaration of Italy stated that the provisions of the Alliance could not be regarded as directed against England.*]

MINISTERIAL DECLARATION

The Royal Italian Government declares that the provisions of the secret Treaty concluded May 20, 1882, between Italy, Austria-Hungary, and Germany, cannot as has been previously agreed, in any case be regarded as being directed against England.

45

THE REINSURANCE TREATY, JUNE 18, 1887 [77]

Aware of Germany's strategic weakness on her exposed eastern frontier, Bismarck was certain that no diplomatic arrangements could be complete without Russia. When in 1887, the Dreikaiserbund *(Three Emperors' League) came to an end, because of the clash of Russian and Austrian interests in the Balkans, Alexander III refused to renew it. Bismarck, however, was determined "to keep open the wires from Berlin to St. Petersburg." Without informing his ally, Austria, of his intentions, he negotiated the so-called "Reinsurance Treaty" (1887) with Russia, in which Germany recognized Russian interests in the eastern Balkans. This was typical of Bismarck's mastery of the art of diplomacy: he reasoned that, since he had a secert treaty with Austria directed against Russia, another secret treaty with Russia against Austria would help maintain the peace. The existence of the Reinsurance Treaty was revealed by Bismarck himself after his fall in 1890. William II allowed it to lapse in 1890.*

✓   ✓   ✓

The Imperial Courts of Germany and of Russia, animated by an equal desire to strengthen the general peace by an understanding destined to assure the defensive position of their respective States, have resolved to confirm the agreement established between them by a special arrangement, in view of the expiration on June 15/27, 1887, of the validity of the secret Treaty and Protocol, signed in

[77] Reprinted by permission of the publishers from Alfred F. Pribram, editor, *The Secret Treaties of Austria-Hungary, 1879-1914* (translated by Archibald Cary Coolidge), [Cambridge, Mass.: Harvard University Press, 1920], I, 275-81.

1881 and renewed in 1884 by the three courts of Germany, Russia, and Austria-Hungary.

To this end the two Courts have named as Plenipotentiaries:

His Majesty the Emperor of Germany, King of Prussia, the Sieur Herbert Count Bismarck-Schoenhausen, His Secretary of State in the Department of Foreign Affairs;

His Majesty the Emperor of All the Russians, the Sieur Paul Count Schouvaloff, His Ambassador Extraordinary and Plenipotentiary to His Majesty the Emperor of Germany, King of Prussia, who, being furnished with full powers, which have been found in good and due form, have agreed upon the following articles:

ARTICLE 1. In case one of the High Contracting Parties should find itself at war with a third Great Power, the other would maintain a benevolent neutrality towards it, and would devote its efforts to the localization of the conflict. This provision would not apply to a war against Austria or France in case this war should result from an attack directed against one of these two latter Powers by one of the High Contracting Parties.

ARTICLE 2. Germany recognizes the rights historically acquired by Russia in the Balkan Peninsula, and particularly the legitimacy of her preponderant and decisive influence in Bulgaria and in Eastern Rumelia. The two Courts engage to admit no modification of the territorial status quo of the said peninsula without a previous agreement between them, and to oppose, as occasion arises, every attempt to disturb this status quo or to modify it without their consent.

ARTICLE 3. The two Courts recognize the European and mutually obligatory character of the principle of the closing of the Straits of the Bosporus and of the Dardanelles, founded on international law, confirmed by treaties, and summed up in the declaration of the second Plenipotentiary of Russia at the session of July 12 of the Congress of Berlin (Protocol 19).

They will take care in common that Turkey shall make no exception to this rule in favor of the interests of any Government whatsoever, by lending to warlike operations of a belligerent power the portion of its Empire constituted by the Straits. In case of infringement, or to prevent it if such infringement should be in prospect, the two Courts will inform Turkey that they would regard her, in that event, as putting herself in a state of war towards the injured Party, and as depriving herself thenceforth of the benefits of the security assured to her territorial status quo by the Treaty of Berlin.

ARTICLE 4. The present Treaty shall remain in force for the space of three years, dating from the day of the exchange of ratifications.

ARTICLE 5. The High Contracting Parties mutually promise secrecy as to the contents and the existence of the present Treaty and of the Protocol annexed thereto.

ARTICLE 6. The present Treaty shall be ratified and ratifications shall be exchanged at Berlin within a period of a fortnight, or sooner it may be.

In witness whereof the respective Plenipotentiaries have signed the present Treaty and have affixed thereto the seal of their arms.

Done at Berlin, the eighteenth day of the month of June, one thousand eight hundred and eighty-seven.

(L.S.) COUNT BISMARCK
(L.S.) COUNT PAUL SCHOUVALOFF

ADDITIONAL PROTOCOL. BERLIN, JUNE 18, 1887

In order to complete the stipulations of Articles 2 and 3 of the secret Treaty concluded on this same date, the two Courts have come to an agreement upon the following points:

1. Germany, as in the past, will lend her assistance to Russia in order to reëstablish a regular and legal government in Bulgaria. She promises in no case to give her consent to the restoration of the Prince of Battenberg.

2. In case His Majesty the Emperor of Russia should find himself under the necessity of assuming the task of defending the entrance of the Black Sea in order to safeguard the interests of Russia, Germany engages to accord her benevolent neutrality and her moral and diplomatic support to the measures which His Majesty may deem it necessary to take to guard the key of His Empire.

3. The present Protocol forms an integral part of the

secret Treaty signed on this day at Berlin, and shall have the same force and validity.

In witness whereof the respective Plenipotentiaries have signed it and have affixed thereto the seal of their arms.

Done at Berlin, the eighteenth day of the month of June, one thousand eight hundred and eighty-seven.

COUNT BISMARCK
COUNT PAUL SCHOUVALOFF

— 46 —

BISMARCK'S DISMISSAL, MARCH, 1890

The chief cause of differences on the domestic scene between the young emperor, William II, and Bismarck arose regarding the prolongation of the law against the Socialists when the bill expired in 1890. Bismarck proposed to make it permanent, but William was opposed to this step on the ground that the disaffection of labor could be removed by remedial measures. In foreign policy, Bismarck hoped to renew the Reinsurance Treaty with Russia, which was due to expire also in 1890, while the Emperor was eager to draw closer to England. In addition, the youthful monarch was fearful that Bismarck intended to create the first of a "Bismarck dynasty" in the person of his son, Herbert, whom he hoped to succeed him in his important political posts.

The matter came to a head on a difference of constitutional principle. When Bismarck heard that the Emperor, on several occasions, had discussed questions of administration with his colleagues without informing him, he drew the attention of the Emperor to a Cabinet order of

*1852, which was enacted as a means of giving the Minis-
ter-President the complete control that was necessary if
he was to be responsible for the whole policy of the government. William replied by commanding that Bismarck
should draw up a new order reversing this decree. In effect, the proposal was to take away from the Chancellor
the supreme position that he had enjoyed for so long. Unable to countenance what he regarded as a degradation of
his position, Bismarck declined to obey the command. Although attempts were made to describe the event as a
resignation, actually, in view of William's repeated demands, it was a dismissal.*

*The first of the following three documents gives the
cabinet order of 1852 which Bismarck regarded as indis-
pensable for his posts. The second contains excerpts from
Bismarck's long letter of resignation. Although couched
in stiffly formal language with expressions of loyalty and
sincerity, it could not hide the bitter hatred of the old
Chancellor for his arrogant young sovereign. The third
document is the text of the order by which William re-
versed the ordinance of 1852.*

✓   ✓   ✓

A

The Cabinet Order of 1852 [78]

I find it imperative that the Minister-President, in order
to maintain a more than hitherto general view over the
various branches of domestic administration (thus making
possible, according to his position, a unity of action),
should give me information on all important administrative measures on my demand. For this purpose I have
decided on the following procedures:

1. On all important administrative measures, which, according to existing regulations, do not require a preliminary decree of the Ministry of State, the respective department chief must come to an understanding, either
orally or in writing, with the Minister-President. The
Minister-President may feel free, according to his judg-

---

[78] Adapted from Freiherr von Eppstein, *Fürst Bismarcks
Entlassung* (Berlin, 1920), note 62.

ment, to call a consultation in the Ministry of State and, also, may deem it advisable to report on it to me.

2. When the administrative measure is such, according to existing regulations, that it necessitates my approval, then the requisite report must be submitted beforehand to the Minister-President, who, with whatever remarks he cares to make, shall place it before me.

3. If a department chief finds it necessary to obtain an audience with me in a matter of immediate importance, he must inform the Minister-President beforehand in time enough so that the latter, if he finds it necessary, can attend the conference personally.—The regular audiences of the War Minister are exempted from this order.

Charlottenburg, September 8, 1852

FRIEDRICH WILHELM
MANTEUFFEL

B

Excerpts from Bismarck's Letter of Resignation, March 18, 1890 [79]

At my respectful audience on the 15th of this month Your Majesty commanded me to draw up a decree annulling the All-Highest Order of September 8, 1852, which regulated the position of the Minister-President vis-à-vis his colleagues.

May I, your humble and most obedient servant, make the following statement on the genesis and importance of this order:

There was no need at that time of absolute monarchy for the position of a "President of the State Ministry." For the first time, in the United Landtag of 1847, the efforts of the liberal delegate (Mevissen) led to the designation, based on the constitutional needs of that day, of a "Premier-President," whose task it would be to supervise uniform policies of the responsible ministers and to take over responsibility for the combined political actions of the cabinet. With the year 1848 came constitutional customs into our daily life, and a "President of the State

[79] Otto von Bismarck, *Gedanken und Erinnerungen* (3 vols.; Stuttgart and Berlin, 1898, 1919) III, 650-54, *passim.*

Ministry" was named. . . . The relationship of the State Ministry and its individual members to the new institution of the Minister-President very quickly required a new constitutional regulation, which was effected with approval of the then State Ministry by the order of September 8, 1852. Since then, this order has been decisive in regulating the relationship of the Minister-President and the State Ministry, and it alone gave the Minister-President the authority which enabled him to take over responsibility for the policies of the cabinet, a responsibility demanded by the *Landtag* as well as public opinion. If each individual minister must receive instructions from the monarch, without previous understandings with his colleagues, it becomes impossible in the cabinet to sustain uniform policies, for which each member can be responsible. There remains for none of the ministers and, especially, for the Minister-President any possibility of bearing constitutional responsibility for the whole policy of the cabinet. . . .

To this time I have never felt the need, in my relationships with my colleagues, to draw upon the order of 1852. Its very existence and the knowledge that I possessed the confidence of their late Majesties, William and Frederick, were enough to assure my authority on my staff. This knowledge exists today neither for my colleagues nor for myself. I have been compelled, therefore, to turn back to the order of 1852, in order to assure the necessary uniformity in the service of Your Majesty.

On the aforementioned grounds, I am not in a position to carry out Your Majesty's demand, which would require me to initiate and countersign the suspension of the order of 1852 recently brought up by me, and, despite that, at the same time carry on the presidency of the Ministry of State. . . .

Considering my attachment to service for the monarchy and for Your Majesty and the long-established relationship which I had believed would exist forever, it is very painful for me to terminate my accustomed relationship to the All Highest and to the political life of the Reich and Prussia; but, after conscientious consideration of the All Highest's intentions, to whose implementation I must always be ready to act, if I am to remain in service, I cannot do other than most humbly request Your Majesty *to grant me an honorable discharge with legal pension from the posts of Reichs-Chancellor, Minister-President, and Prussian Minister for Foreign Affairs.* . . .

VON BISMARCK

To His Majesty the Emperor and King

C

William II's Suspension of the Order of 1852 [80]

Since the utilization of the order of September 8, 1852 by His late Majesty the King, Frederick William IV, concerning the relationships of the President of my State Ministry and the State Ministry itself, has given rise to doubts, I decree the suspension of this order under the following considerations:

It is the task of the President of my State Ministry to bear the responsibility for the uniform and equal implementation of the basic principles decided by myself as authoritative for the guidance of all administration. In order to fulfill this task, it is imperative that the department chiefs, after previous understanding with the President of my State Ministry, obtain my decision on all matters which diverge from the abovementioned basic principles, or which are of essential importance. Where there are differences of opinion, both the Minister-President and the department chief are to come to me in common audience. At the same time, I want to clarify my order of May 2, 1889 by noting that, in cases where members of my State Ministry are concerned with changes or the initiation of proposals which reach the parliamentary bodies for debate, the aforementioned obtaining of my decision shall be required only in so far as the point of view represents a divergence from the basic principles approved by me or follows a direction which casts doubt on my interpretation.

WILHELM R.
CAPRIVI

[80] Cabinet Order of April 14, 1890, quoted in O. Gradenowitz, *Bismarcks letzter Kampf, 1888-1898, Skizzen nach Akten* (Berlin, 1924), p. 114.

RERUM NOVARUM: POPE LEO XIII ON THE SOCIAL ORDER, MAY 15, 1891 [81]

The problems of the Industrial Revolution led to the formation of a Catholic "social" movement designed to combat economic liberalism on the one hand and Marxian socialism on the other, while aiming at the Christianization of modern industrial society. On May 15, 1891, Pope Leo XIII issued a famous encyclical, the Rerum Novarum, which won for him the title of "the workingman's Pope." The document denounced Marxian Socialism as violating the natural right to property and as inciting to class hatred, stressed the importance of the family, protested against exaltation of the state, and condemned the doctrine of economic determinism. The solution to the social problem, said the Pope, was to be found in harmonious relations between capital and labor. He urged workmen to be peaceful and loyal to their employers, and, at the same time, advised the latter to treat their workers as Christian freemen and not to exploit them as slaves. The pontiff called for a wider distribution of private property, the fostering of industrial trade unions, and the restriction of hours of employment, especially of women and children. He emphasized, above all, the place of the Church in bringing about a better social order.

The Rerum Novarum stimulated the formation throughout Europe of Catholic trade unions, which won a following second only to those of the Socialists. Following are extracts from this important encyclical.

[81] Encyclical Letter of Pope Leo XIII, text in The American Catholic Quarterly Review, XVI (July, 1891), 529-57, passim.

Encyclical Letter of Pope Leo XIII
To Our Venerable Brethren, All Patriarchs,
Primates, Archbishops, and Bishops of the
Catholic World, in Grace and Communion
with the Apostolic See

Venerable Brethren, Health and Apostolic Benediction.

It is not surprising that the spirit of revolutionary change, which has been so long predominant in the nations of the world, should have passed beyond politics and made its influence felt in the cognate field of practical economy. The elements of a conflict are unmistakable; the growth of industry, and the surprising discoveries of science; the changed relations of masters and workmen; the enormous fortunes of individuals, and the poverty of the masses; the increased self-reliance and the closer mutual combination of the working population; and, finally, a general moral deterioration. The momentous seriousness of the present state of things just now fills every mind with painful apprehension; wise men discuss it, practical men propose schemes; popular meetings, legislatures, and sovereign princes, all are occupied with it—and there is nothing which has a deeper hold on public attention.

Therefore, Venerable Brethren, as on former occasions, when it seemed opportune to refute false teaching, We have addressed you in the interests of the Church and of the common weal, and have issued Letters on Political Power, on Human Liberty, on the Christian Constitution of the State, and on similar subjects, so now We have thought it useful to speak on the Condition of Labor. . . . The discussion is not easy, nor is it free from danger. It is not easy to define the relative rights and the mutual duties of the wealthy and of the poor, of capital and labor. And the danger lies in this, that crafty agitators constantly make use of these disputes to pervert men's judgments and to stir up the people to sedition.

. . . By degrees it has come to pass that Working Men have been given over, isolated and defenceless, to the callousness of employers and the greed of unrestrained competition. The evil has been increased by rapacious Usury, which, although more than once condemned by the Church, is, nevertheless, under a different form but with the same

guilt, still practised by avaricious and grasping men. And
to this must be added the custom of working by contract,
and the concentration of so many branches of trade in the
hands of a few individuals, so that a small number of very
rich men have been able to lay upon the masses of the
poor a yoke a little better than slavery itself.

To remedy these evils the *Socialists,* working on the
poor man's envy of the rich, endeavor to destroy private
property, and maintain that individual possessions should
become the common property of all, to be administered by
the State or by municipal bodies. . . . But their proposals
are so clearly futile for all practical purposes, that if they
were carried out the working man himself would be
among the first to suffer. Moreover, they are emphatically
unjust, because they would rob the lawful possessor, bring
the State into a sphere that is not its own, and cause complete confusion in the community. . . .

It is clear that the main tenet of *Socialism,* the community of goods, must be utterly rejected; for it would
injure those whom it is intended to benefit; it would be
contrary to the natural rights of mankind, and it would
introduce confusion and disorder into the commonwealth.
Our first and most fundamental principle, therefore, when
we undertake to alleviate the condition of the masses, must
be the inviolability of private property. . . .

No practical solution of this question will ever be found
without the assistance of Religion and of the Church. It
is We who are the chief guardian of Religion and the
chief dispenser of what belongs to the Church, and We
must not by silence neglect the duty which lies upon
Us. . . .

If Christian precepts prevail the two classes [*rich and
poor*] will not only be united in the bonds of friendship,
but also in those of brotherly love. For they will understand and feel that all men are the children of the common Father, that is, of God; that all have the same last
end, which is God himself, who alone can make either
men or angels absolutely and perfectly happy; that all and
each are redeemed by Jesus Christ and raised to the dignity of children of God, and are thus united in brotherly
ties both with each other and with Jesus Christ, *the first-
born among many brethren;* that the blessings of nature

and the gifts of grace belong in common to the whole human race, and that to all, except to those who are unworthy, is promised the inheritance of the Kingdom of Heaven. *If sons, heirs also; heirs indeed of God, and co-heirs of Christ.* (*Romans,* viii, 171.)

Such is the scheme of duties and rights which is put forth to the world by the Gospel. Would it not seem that strife must quickly cease were society penetrated with ideas like these? . . .

As far as regards the Church, its assistance will never be wanting, be the time or the occasion what it may; and it will intervene with the greater effect in proportion as its liberty of action is the more unfettered: let this be carefully noted by those whose office it is to provide for the public welfare. Every minister of holy Religion must throw into the conflict all the energy of his mind and all the strength of his endurance. With your authority, Venerable Brethren, and by your example, they must never cease to urge upon all men of every class, upon the high as well as the lowly, the Gospel doctrines of Christian life; by every means in their power they must strive for the good of the people; and above all they must earnestly cherish in themselves, and try to arouse in others, Charity, the mistress and queen of virtues. For the happy results we all long for must be chiefly brought about by the plenteous outpouring of Charity; of that true Christian Charity which is the fulfilling of the whole Gospel law, which is always ready to sacrifice itself for others' sake, and which is man's surest antidote against worldly pride and immoderate love of self; that Charity, whose office is described and whose Godlike features are drawn by the Apostle St. Paul in these words: *Charity is patient, is kind . . . seeketh not her own . . . suffereth all things . . . endureth all things.* (*I. Corinthians,* xiii, 4-7.)

On each of you, Venerable Brethren, and your clergy and people, as an earnest of God's mercy and a mark of our affection, We lovingly in the Lord bestow the Apostolic Benediction.

Given at St. Peter's, in Rome, the fifteenth day of May, 1891, the fourteenth year of Our Pontificate.

LEO XIII., POPE

48

THE FRANCO-RUSSIAN ALLIANCE MILITARY CONVENTION, AUGUST 18, 1892 [82]

The Bismarckian treaty system maintained Germany's position as the strongest power on the Continent for some time. Meanwhile, a reaction gradually set in, as France, Russia, and England settled their differences and concluded a set of agreements leading to the Triple Entente of 1907. The first stage was an alliance between democratic France and autocratic Russia—between Europe's youngest republic and her oldest empire. The general understanding took definite form in the Military Convention of August, 1892, signed by the French and Russian Chiefs of Staff. In January, 1894, it was given binding effect by an exchange of diplomatic notes, thereby attaining the force of a treaty. The Military Convention was not made public until 1918. This alliance was followed in 1904 by the Entente Cordiale between England and France and the Anglo-Russian Entente of 1907, all of which formed the coalition of the Triple Entente. By providing for mutual assistance in the event of war with any of the Central Powers, the Triple Entente served as a counteracting force to the Triple Alliance.

✓　　　　　✓　　　　　✓

France and Russia, being animated by a common desire to preserve peace, and having no other object than to meet the necessities of a defensive war, provoked by an attack of the forces of the Triple Alliance against either of them, have agreed upon the following provisions:

1. If France is attacked by Germany, or by Italy sup-

[82] *Ministère des affaires étrangères. Documents diplomatiques. L'Alliance Franco-Russe* (Paris, 1918), No. 71, p. 92. Translated by the editor.

ported by Germany, Russia shall employ all her available forces to attack Germany.

If Russia is attacked by Germany, or by Austria supported by Germany, France shall employ all her available forces to attack Germany.

2. In case the forces of the Triple Alliance, or of any one of the Powers belonging to it, should be mobilized, France and Russia, at the first news of this event and without previous agreement being necessary, shall mobilize immediately and simultaneously the whole of their forces, and shall transport them as far as possible to their frontiers.

3. The available forces to be employed against Germany shall be, on the part of France, 1,300,000 men, on the part of Russia, 700,000 or 800,000 men.

These forces shall engage to the full with such speed that Germany will have to fight simultaneously on the East and on the West.

4. The General Staffs of the Armies of the two countries shall coöperate with each other at all times in the preparation and facilitation of the execution of the measures mentioned above.

They shall communicate with each other, while there is still peace, all information relative to the armies of the Triple Alliance which is already in their possession or shall come into their possession.

Ways and means of corresponding in time of war shall be studied and worked out in advance.

5. France and Russia shall not conclude peace separately.

6. The present Convention shall have the same duration as the Triple Alliance.

7. All the clauses enumerated above shall be kept absolutely secret.

Signature of the Minister :

Signature of the Minister :

General Aide-de-Camp Chief of the General Staff
Signed: OBRUCHEFF

General of Division, Councillor of State
Sub-Chief of the General Staff of the Army
Signed: BOISDEFFRE

49

ZOLA'S "J'ACCUSE," JANUARY 13, 1898 [83]

On the surface the Dreyfus affair appeared to be an imbroglio of what Thomas Carlyle would have called "despicable personalities," but actually it was a significant chapter in the history of France. In the fall of 1894, Alfred Dreyfus, a captain of artillery attached to the French General Staff, was arrested and accused of having sold important French military secrets to the Germans. On being found guilty by a court-martial, he was stripped of his commission in a public degradation and condemned to solitary confinement on Devil's Island, a notorious convict settlement near French Guiana.

Dreyfus was a Jew. Many bigoted French nationalists, seeking a scapegoat for their country's troubles, derived considerable satisfaction from the conviction of the Jewish officer. The real issue, it appeared, was the maintenance of a caste system, not only in the army, but in French society. Various political factions rallied to one side or the other. Monarchists, clericals, and anti-Semites joined hands to contend that Dreyfus was guilty.

The complicating and disturbing factor was that Dreyfus was innocent. A saving factor in an incredibly nasty situation—the railroading of an innocent man—was the admirable behavior of a group of distinguished Frenchmen— Émile Zola, Jean Jaurès, Georges Clemenceau, and Anatole France—who had a jealous regard for the honor of their country. Zola, who had known success as a novelist, was fascinated by the case of the Jewish captain that was convulsing French politics and social life. Several days after the acquittal of the real culprit, Esterhazy, Zola published in the newspaper L'Aurore an impassioned letter addressed to the President of the Republic. "It was a breast bared," wrote one observer, "an indignant conscience calling other consciences to its aid." To Anatole France it was "a moment in the conscience of mankind."

[83] *L'Aurore*, January 13, 1898. Translated by the editor.

For his pains Zola was convicted of libel, his name was struck from the rolls of the Legion of Honor, and he was forced to leave France and live in exile in England for more than a year.

Eventually, Dreyfus was restored to the Army and promoted in rank. Zola died before the affair ended; his remains were buried with great pomp in the Panthéon. The honor of France was vindicated by the dismissal of officers in the case against Dreyfus. The affair turned out to be not a "great Jewish conspiracy" to deliver France to the enemy, but a momentous political battle in which republican and democratic ideas won a striking victory against the forces of reaction.

I ACCUSE . . . !

Letter to the President of the Republic

By Émile Zola

A court-martial has dared, by command, to acquit a man like Esterhazy, thus dealing a supremely insolent blow to all truth and justice. It has been done. France bears this stain upon her cheek. . . . Since they had dared, I shall dare also. . . . It is my duty to speak out. I do not wish to be an accessory. My dreams would be haunted by the specter of an innocent man who is suffering the most frightful agonies for a crime that he did not commit. . . .

Ah! The feebleness of this indictment! It is a monstrous thing that a man should be found guilty on such a charge. I defy any man of honesty to read it without being overcome with indignation and crying out in horror at the thought of the unlimited suffering there on Devil's Island. Dreyfus knows several languages; this is a crime. No compromising papers were found at his house; this is a crime. On occasion he pays a visit to the country of his birth; this is a crime. He is industrious, he wants to know about everything; this is a crime; He is not nervous, a crime; he is nervous, a crime. . . .

It is said that the judges, when they were in the council chamber, were about to acquit him as a matter of course. One can understand the desperation with which, in order

to justify the verdict, it has been said that a secret, irre-
futable document exists. . . . I deny the existence of this
document. I deny it with all my strength . . . It is said
that this document could not be produced without war
being declared tomorrow, no, no! That is a lie. It is all the
more disgusting and cynical because it is a lie told with
impunity and no one is able to refute it. They have stirred
up a hornet's nest in France and are hiding behind her
legitimate emotions; they have closed the mouths, while
disturbing the hearts and crippling the minds of the people. I know of no greater civic crime. . . .

The first court-martial may have been unintelligent, but
the second is actually criminal. Its excuse, I repeat, is that
the supreme chief had declared the thing to be above attack, sacred, superior to man, so that inferiors cannot contradict it. They have spoken to us of the honor of the
army, that we should respect and love it, Ah, yes, indeed,
that army that is ready to rise at the first danger, that
would defend the soil of France, that army which is the
people itself, and we have nothing but respect and tender-
ness for it. However, it is not merely a question of that
army, the dignity of which we seek to maintain, when we
demand justice. It is a matter of the sword, the master
who might possibly be our ruler tomorrow. Shall we de-
voutly kiss the hilt of the sword, the god? No! . . .

It is a crime, while impudently plotting to fool the whole
world, to bring an accusation of disturbing France against
those who desire to recognize her as a noble leader of
free and righteous nations. It is a crime to mislead public
opinion, to make murderous use of that opinion, after
having perverted it to a delirium. It is a crime to poison
the minds of the obscure and humble, to awaken the pas-
sions of intolerance and reaction, while hiding behind the
vile anti-Semitism of which the great liberal France of
the Rights of Man will surely die, if she is not cured of it.
It is a crime to exploit patriotism in the cause of hatred.
And, finally, it is a crime to make a modern god of the
sword, when all human science works in the growing cause
of justice and truth. . . .

When truth is driven underground, it grows and gath-
ers so great an explosive force that, when it finally does
explode, it carries everyone before it. Indeed, we shall see

whether there has not already been prepared—possibly for some future time—the most shocking of disasters.

But this letter has become too long, Mr. President, and it is time to conclude it.

I accuse Lieutenant-Colonel du Paty de Clam of having been the devilish author of this judicial miscarriage of justice—unconsciously, I am ready to believe—and then for three years of having defended his vile work by the most absurd and guilty machinations.

I accuse General Mercier of having made himself the accomplice, certainly by his lack of firmness, of one of the greatest injustices of the century.

I accuse General Billot of having had in his hands certain proofs of the innocence of Dreyfus, and of having kept them quiet, of having made himself guilty of the crime of *lèse-humanité* and *lèse justice* because of political aims and in order to protect the compromised General Staff.

I accuse General de Boisdeffre and General Gonse of having made themselves accomplices of the same crime—the one, without doubt, through clerical prejudice, the other, perhaps, from the *esprit de corps* which makes the War Office a sacred, unassailable ark.

I accuse General de Pellieux and Major Ravary of having made an infamous inquiry, and I mean an inquiry of the most monstrous partiality, a report which is an imperishable monument of naive audacity.

I accuse the three handwriting experts, *Sieurs* Belhomme, Varinard, and Couard, of having made a false and fraudulent report, unless it be found by medical examination that they have been suffering from defective vision and diseased judgment.

I accuse the War Office of having carried on in the press, especially in *Élair* and *Écho de Paris* a rotten campaign to hide its mistakes and to mislead the public.

Finally, I accuse the first court-martial of having violated the law by condemning an accused man on the basis of a secret document. In addition, I accuse the second court-martial of having, in obedience to orders from above, hidden that illegality by committing in its turn the legal crime of knowingly acquitting a guilty man (*Esterhazy*).

In making these charges, I am well aware that I am

bringing myself under Articles 30 and 31 of the Press Law of July 29, 1881, which decrees punishment for libel. I do so voluntarily.

I do not know the men I accuse. I have never seen them. I have no resentment nor enmity toward them. For me they are merely entities, spirits of social evil. And what I am doing here is only a revolutionary means of hastening the revelation of truth and justice.

My only passion is—light. I crave it for the sake of humanity, which has suffered so much and which is entitled to happiness. My passionate protest is just the outcry of my soul. I dare them to bring me before the Court of Assize and make an inquiry in broad daylight!

I wait.

— 50 —

THE OPEN-DOOR POLICY IN CHINA, 1899-1900

The Sino-Japanese War of 1894-95 revealed to the world the political and military weakness of China. One after another the major powers demanded political and economic concessions in China in the form of leaseholds and spheres of influence. In 1898 Germany obtained a ninety-nine year lease on the harbor of Kiao-chao, France "leased" Kwang-chau-wan, England the port of Wei-hai-wei, and Russia held the Manchurian peninsula on a twenty-five year lease with absolute control in the meantime.

The United States, which remained aloof from this imperialistic scramble, considered these events adverse to its trade interests. In both England and the United States there was a growing fear that the encroachments of the

European powers and Japan on China would lead to the destruction of the territorial integrity and sovereignty of China and consequent discrimination against British and American interests there.

These three notes together formed the famous Open Door policy. They should be regarded not as a contribution to the law of nations but rather as an effort to crystallize public opinion.

✓   ✓   ✓

A

Hay's Open-Door Note, September 6, 1899 [84]

Mr. Hay to Mr. White

Department of State
Washington, September 6, 1899

Sir: At the time when the Government of the United States was informed by that of Germany that it had leased from His Majesy the Emperor of China the port of Kiao-chao and the adjacent territory in the province of Shan-tung, assurances were given to the ambassador of the United States at Berlin by the Imperial German minister for foreign affairs that the rights and privileges insured by treaties with China to citizens of the United States would not thereby suffer or be in anywise impaired within the area over which Germany has thus obtained control.

More recently, however, the British Government recognized by a formal agreement with Germany the exclusive right of the latter country to enjoy in said leased area and the contiguous "sphere of influence or interest" certain privileges, more especially those relating to railroads and mining enterprises; but, as the exact nature and extent of the rights thus recognized have not been clearly defined, it is possible that serious conflicts of interest may at any time arise, not only between British and German subjects within said area, but that the interests of our citizens may also be jeopardized.

[84] William W. Malloy, ed., *Treaties, Conventions, International Acts, Protocols and Agreements between the United States of America and other Powers* (3 vols., Washington, 1910-23), I, 246.

Earnestly desirous to remove any cause of irritation and to insure at the same time to the commerce of all nations in China the undoubted benefits which should accrue from a formal recognition by the various powers claiming "spheres of interest" that they shall enjoy perfect equality of treatment for their commerce and navigation within such "spheres," the Government of the United States would be pleased to see His German Majesty's Government give formal assurances and lend its coöperation in securing like assurances from the other interested powers that each within its respective sphere of whatever influence—

First. Will in no way interfere with any treaty port or any vested interest within any so-called "sphere of interest" or leased territory it may have in China.

Second. That the Chinest treaty tariff of the time being shall apply to all merchandise landed or shipped to all such ports as are within said "sphere of interest" (unless they be "free ports"), no matter to what nationality it may belong, and that duties so levitable shall be collected by the Chinese Government.

Third. That it will levy no higher harbor dues on vessels of another nationality frequenting any such port in such "sphere" than shall be levied on vessels of its own nationality. . . .

Copy of this instruction is sent to our ambassadors at London and at St. Petersburg for their information.

I have, etc.,

JOHN HAY

B

Hay's Letter of Instruction, March 20, 1900 [85]

Instructions sent mutatus mutandis *to the United States ambassadors at London, Paris, Berlin, St. Petersburg, and Rome, and to the United States Minister at Tokyo.*

Department of State
Washington, March 20, 1900

Sir: The ——— Government having accepted the declaration suggested by the United States concerning for-

[85] Malloy, *op. cit.*, I, 260.

eign trade in China, the terms of which I transmitted to you in my instruction No. —— of ——, and like action having been taken by all the various powers having leased territory or so-called "spheres of interest" in the Chinese Empire, as shown by the notes which I herewith transmit to you, you will please inform the government to which you are accredited, that the condition originally attached to its acceptance—that all other powers concerned should likewise accept the proposals of the United States—having been complied with, this Government will therefore consider the assent given to it by —— as final and definitive.

You will also transmit to the minister of foreign affairs copies of the present inclosures, and by the same occasion convey to him the expression of the sincere gratification which the President feels at the successful termination of these negotiations, in which he sees proof of the friendly spirit which animates the various powers interested in the untrammeled development of commerce and industry in the Chinese Empire and a source of vast benefit to the whole commercial world.

I am, etc.,

JOHN HAY

C

Hay's Circular Letter, July 3, 1900 [86]

Circular telegram sent to the United States embassies in Berlin, Paris, London, Rome, and St. Petersburg, and to the United States missions in Vienna, Brussels, Madrid, Tokyo, The Hague, and Lisbon.

Department of State
Washington, July 3, 1900

In this critical posture of affairs in China it is deemed appropriate to define the attitude of the United States as far as present circumstances permit this to be done. We adhere to the policy initiated by us in 1857, of peace with the Chinese nation, of furtherance of lawful commerce, and of protection of lives and property of our citizens by all means guaranteed under extraterritorial treaty rights and by the law of nations. If wrong be done our citizens

[86] *Foreign Relations of the United States, 1900,* p. 345.